P9-EDV-001

THE PRODUCTIONS OF TIME

•

Eternity is in love with
the Productions of Time
(Wm. Blake)

THE PRODUCTIONS OF TIME:

TRADITION HISTORY IN OLD TESTAMENT SCHOLARSHIP

•

Edited by
Knud Jeppesen & Benedikt Otzen

•

A Symposium
at Sandbjerg Manor, Denmark
May 1982

Published for
The Department of Old Testament Studies
University of Aarhus
by

The Almond Press · 1984

Translated from the original manuscripts
in Norwegian, Swedish, German, and Danish
by
Frederick H.Cryer MA

•

ISBN 0 907459 36 6 Hardback
ISBN 0 907459 37 4 Paperback

BS
1171,2
,P73
1984
/ 72675
•

Copyright © 1984 The Almond Press

Published by
The Almond Press
P.O. Box 208
Sheffield S10 5DW
England

Printed in Great Britain by
Dotesios (Printers) Ltd
Bradford-on-Avon, Wiltshire
1984

TABLE OF CONTENTS

AUGUSTANA UNIVERSITY COLLEGE
LIBRARY

To
professor dr. phil. et theol.
Erling Hammershaimb
on the occasion of his
eightieth birthday.

PREFACE

In May 24-27, 1982, the Institute for Old Testament Study of Aarhus University arranged a Nordic Symposium on Old Testament research. It took place at Sandbjerg Manor, which is depicted on the dustjacket of this volume; it is situated near Sønderborg in the southernmost reaches of Jutland, not far from the present border between Denmark and Germany. The Manor belongs to Aarhus University, having been donated to the University by a philanthropist back in the nineteen-fifties; it now serves as a conference centre. The Manor is in the midst of a very beautiful countryside, in a region which has been witness to warfare many times, the most recent occasion being in the last century when the borders between Scandinavia and Germany once again had to be defended and redefined. This was the heyday of political Scandinavianism, and it was also on this last occasion and in this region that Scandinavianism suffered its ultimate defeat.

Half a hundred Scandinavian Old Testament scholars representing the theological faculties of Lund, Uppsala, Chicago, Oslo (including both the State and Congregational faculties), Helsinki, Åbo Academy, Reykjavik, Copenhagen, and Aarhus assembled at Sandbjerg to determine whether Old Testament Scandinavianism had also suffered a defeat, or whether there were still signs of life.

The participants attended lectures on subjects central to Old Testament research; these were followed up by engaging discussions. This volume contains the lectures presented on this occasion in the order in which they were delivered. All of them deal with tradition history in its Scandinavian dress from a variety of vantage points. We conclude with a brief characterization of the discussions which took place in conjunction with the various addresses.

By way of introduction, we had requested Prof. G. Gerleman of Lund to lecture on a subject of his own choice. This was in gratitude to Prof. Gerleman for his own contributions in having assembled Nordic Old Testament scholars for similar symposia in Vittsjö (1968 and 1975). Prof. Gerleman lectured on "The Son of Man" at Sandbjerg; his conclusions are now available in his newly-released work, *Der Menschensohn*, Leiden 1983.

This collection is dedicated to Prof. Erling Hammershaimb of Aarhus, on the occasion of his eightieth birthday on the 4th of March, 1984. Prof. Hammershaimb is the real founder of the Institute for Old

Testament Study at Aarhus University. In presenting an examination
of this kind into the status of Scandinavian research in Prof. Hammershaimb's field, we thus take the occasion to thank him for his
contributions in this area, as well as for the inspiration he has above
all provided to our Institute.

Institut for Gammel Testamente
Aarhus Universitet

The contributions to this volume are translated from the original manuscripts in Norwegian, Swedish, German, and Danish by our colleague Frederick Cryer, who also made the index. The editors want
to express their gratefulness to him for his help, and to the secretary
of the department, Mrs. Birgit Herman Hansen; without her effort the
symposium would neither have taken place nor would this volume
have been published.

The editors

THE TRADITIO-HISTORICAL STUDY OF THE PENTATEUCH SINCE 1945, WITH SPECIAL EMPHASIS ON SCANDINAVIA

Eduard Nielsen

Introduction

The title of this paper has been formulated in such a way that at some point one would expect to hear the name Ivan Engnell mentioned. Engnell's *Gamla Testamentet, I, En traditionshistorisk Inledning* appeared in 1945, and the last chapter of this work (pp. 168-259), while also cursorily covering the Deuteronomistic and Chronistic Histories, was primarily devoted to the Pentateuch.

Here it will be necessary briefly to regress in order to indicate some of the presuppositions for the development of post-war Pentateuch research especially in Scandinavia. It will not be necessary to mention such figures as H.B. Witter, J. Astruc, Graf or Wellhausen, nor, for that matter, even Gunkel or Gressmann. Rather, it is sufficient to point to the three *grand old men* of Scandinavia whose researches, incidentally, extended all the way into the 1960's: Norway's Sigmund Mowinckel, Sweden's Johs. Lindblom, and Denmark's Johs. Pedersen. These three scholars made pioneering contributions to the study of Old Testament literature in areas where Engnell was subsequently to develop his traditio-historical insights. Mowinckel's contribution was mainly in the understanding of the Psalms. Johs. Lindblom's was in the study of prophecy, while Johs. Pedersen studied the epic and legal materials. From all three Engnell (and, independently of him, many others) received enduring impressions. Admittedly, Engnell's relationship to his three masters varied in degree of enthusiasm: he ranged from cool to polemical towards Mowinckel, respectful and judicious towards Johs. Lindblom, and unconditionally admiring towards Johs.

11

Pedersen. A fourth master of significance for Engnell was the local "outsider", H.S. Nyberg, especially because of the latter's studies of syncretism during the Monarchy (Studien zum Religionskampf im Alten Testament, 1938, *Hoseaboken*, 1941), and of oral tradition (*Studien zum Hoseabuche*, 1935). The last-mentioned of these had called for a more moderate form of Old Testament text criticism and for more confidence in the Massoretic text, a point at which the views of Nyberg and Johs. Pedersen coincided perfectly.

Johs. Lindblom's works prior to 1945 are not especially relevant to my purpose here, while Mowinckel's certainly are. His book on the Decalogue (Mowinckel 1927) was of crucial significance thanks to his comprehensive analysis of legal and narrative materials from Exod 19-24 and 32-34 and of Old Testament cultic poetry, and because of his attempts to demonstrate a cultic *Sitz im Leben* for the religio-moral teaching which received its classical expression in the Ten Commandments. One could also mention Mowinckel's studies on the Balaam narrative, which appeared in both Norwegian and German (1930 a and b). Quite in the tradition of Gunkel and Gressmann, these studies begin with classical source criticism, but their main emphasis nevertheless consists in that aspect which has come to be designated *tradition history* or *Überlieferungsgeschichte*. Mowinckel's contributions to *GTMMM*, I (1929) ought perhaps also to be mentioned in this connexion, as they, too, demonstrate how solid his attachment was to the time-hallowed methods of source- and text criticism, despite his openness to new directions. As is well known, Mowinckel adhered until his death to the theory of a J-source, whose conclusion he found in Judg 1, a P-source whose author was seen to be both narrator and compiler of laws, and a D-source. Mowinckel's suggested datings for these materials are interesting by reason of their radicality: he held J to be no older than 800 (the reign of Amaziah), and D and P to be both post-exilic. As far as the date of D was concerned, Mowinckel was clearly dependent on G. Hölscher (1942), but support for this view was also to be had from Johs. Pedersen. The importation of the theory about the significance of "oral tradition" into Norway by Harris Birkeland (1938) led Mowinckel to abandon the notion of an E-source in fixed (i.e. written) form running parallel to J. Instead, he suggested that some of J's materials had survived orally for some time after J was written down; these materials will then have been transmitted in Judaean circles, and Mowinckel designated them J^V, *Jahvista variata*. (1964a; 1964b; 1967).

But for tradition history proper, as it was propounded by Engnell, in part in his *Inledning*, in part in various articles in *Svenskt Bibliskt Uppslagsverk*, which Engnell edited together with his old New Testament teacher, Anton Fridrichsen, from 1948-1952, Johs. Pedersen's influence proved to be greater than Mowinckel's, and for a number of reasons. First, there was Pedersen's conscious break with literary criticism and his theory concerning the cultic basis of the Passover legend; second, his reluctance to tamper with the transmitted Hebrew text; and finally, and not least important, was Pedersen's demonstration of the profound influence exercised by Canaanite culture on the Israelite people. As for Pedersen's criticism of the documentary hypothesis, it is sufficient to note that he was of the opinion that source-critical work was overly preoccupied with peripheral concerns and that it was often founded on assumptions deriving from modern Western evolutionary ideas. Against these tendencies Pedersen held a sensitive psychological exploration of the materials to be essential to the understanding of the Old Testament texts. As far as the dating of these so-called "sources" was concerned, he asserted that they were both pre- and post-exilic, and that the decisive break in the Israelites' cultural history first occurred when Judaism was exposed to the influence of Hellenism. This does not mean that Pedersen rejected the thought of development within Israelite culture. In fact, he presented a developmental sketch in *Israel*, III-IV (1934), and if we compare this with, for example, Wellhausen's *Israelitische und Jüdische Geschichte* (1894), the distance between these two works is not insuperable. Moreover, it should also be remarked that in his evaluation of the texts illuminated in *Israel* Pedersen is in agreement with the classical source critics more often than one would expect[1]; furthermore, he never really propounded an alternative method himself. Nor can Pedersen's analysis of Exod 1-15 as the festival legend (*hieros logos*) of the Passover (1934a, pp. 545-551; Eng. pp. 728-737; 1934b) ultimately bear the burden of the complexity of the texts, especially if we consider recent research into the Passover. If the Passover did indeed become a true temple or national festival in the period only shortly before the Exile, then the Exodus motif must have had some other basis in pre-exilic times. Of course, this would not rule out the possibility that the Exodus story was the central tradition around which the rest of the Pentateuchal traditions accumulated when they were eventually collected.

Finally, in conclusion to these introductory remarks we shall turn our attention to two of the great names of the 1930's, whose contributions continued on in German scholarship throughout the 40's, 50's and 60's: Gerhard von Rad and Martin Noth. Like Mowinckel, both scholars retained the main elements of the source hypothesis, i.e., a J, D, and P source; but in reality von Rad and Noth were the first seriously to exploit the possibilities of tradition history on German soil. In 1938 von Rad could still entitle his analysis of the structure of the Pentateuch *Das formgeschichtliche Problem des Hexateuchs*, but this is misleading, since form criticism has to do with small units rather than great literary complexes like the entire Pentateuch. Thus Mowinckel correctly noted (1964a, p. 52) that von Rad's title should have read, "Das traditionsgeschichtliche Problem des Hexateuchs". Von Rad's work is so well known that it does not require discussion here, but what makes it a traditio-historical analysis is his study of the collection and structuring of ancient materials around the nucleus of the historical Credo (Deut 26:5ff). Its provisional terminus was the Yahwist's work of history, behind which one senses the age of David and Solomon, the Israelite empire, the Exodus of the twelve tribes and their seizure of the Land, the insertion of the traditions of the covenant on Sinai, and by way of introduction the stories of the patriarchs, with the Primeval History as an ouverture. Von Rad finds the Yahwist's own theological interpretation exactly on the borderline between the Primeval History and the patriarchal narratives at Gen 12:1-3; Abraham's posterity are designated heirs to the blessing. Already in 1938 von Rad suggested that the Yahwist had composed his work during Solomon's "freigeistige Ära", in which the spiritual presuppositions for the Yahwist's contribution were present: it was possible to loosen local traditions from their attachment to the local shrines and to construct from their material a national historical epic[2].

The works of M. Noth which are relevant to our purposes here are his commentary on the Book of Joshua (1938), *Überlieferungsgeschichtliche Studien* I (1943), and *Überlieferungsgeschichte des Pentateuch* (1948). For reasons of space I will limit my remarks to the two first-named works. Noth's studies in depth in his Joshua commentary of topographical details and etiologies, borderlines, and lists of cities and districts led him as an historian to abandon one of the most widely acknowledged axioms of source criticism, namely, that J and P were present in the Book of Joshua. Of course, this conclusion implied that one might be forced to reject the major premiss of von Rad's structural model, that is, that the Yahwist, being the fundamental source of the Pentateuch, had consciously aimed at the *Landnahme* by including a narrative about the conquest which served to legitimate the people's sovereignty over Canaan. Alternatively, however, it was possible to hold that while such a narrative might once have existed, it was eventually expurgated in favour of other traditions. In his work which appeared in 1943, Noth promulgated the thesis that Gen-Num (comprised of J, E and P) was a finished work which had been secondarily united with the Deuteronomistic Historical Work. This work began with Deut 1 and ended at 2 Kgs 25; its original form was the work of a single author who probably lived north of Jerusalem in the tribal territory of Benjamin or Ephraim and wrote around 550. Thus the historical retrospect found in Deut 1-3 is not the introduction to Deuteronomy as such, but to the entire Historical Work. The link-up with Gen-Num was redactionally completed by the insertion of P's account of the death of Moses into Deut 34, or, if you will, one could say that Deut 1-33 was placed just prior to P's narrative of Moses' death and was thus separated from its actual continuation in Josh 1 by a couple of verses from the P source.

We may now return to Scandinavia in 1945.

Engnell

Engnell's *Gamla Testamentet* (1945) begins with two relatively short, not to say thin, chapters dealing witht the histories of Canon and Text, followed in Ch. III (pp. 39-108) by a discussion of literary forms in which the author develops his traditio-historical views, strongly emphasizes the role of oral tradition, and equally forcefully dismisses literary-critical methods. In the section on *poetry* he remarks (p. 68) that Job, the Ebed-Yahweh songs, Proverbs and Ecclesiastes are literary works whose roots are ultimately to be sought in the Royal Psalms, and which are examples of the "disintegration" and "democratization" of Israelite ideology and religion. The remark is significant in that it reveals both Engnell's overarching concern with the phenomenology of religion and the inspiration provided by the Myth-and-Ritual School (cf. Hooke 1933; 1935). This concern, as well as the inspiration from the Myth-and-Ritual School retained their hold on Engnell throughout his career and indeed sometimes violently influenced his contributions to *SBU*. As far as the *prose* is concerned, Engnell's evaluation of the religious pragmatism of Israelite historical writing is noteworthy in that he holds that the reason for such pragmatism must have resided in Israel's historical experiences and singular religious faith. But to this he adds that it is difficult to accept the view that already the most ancient traditions (the J and E of literary criticism) fully embody this religious pragmatism that so completely dominates the final form of the materials. Rather, Engnell holds that this view was first incorporated during the final redaction of the texts in the fifth century, even if the religious-pragmatic understanding of history as such was much older. The author cites with approval Johs. Pedersen's statement that, "The more the self-confidence of the people was shaken, the more it clung to its history" (Pedersen 1934a, p.505; cf. Eng. p. 668).

While Engnell's history-of-religions survey in Ch. IV (pp. 109-167) is of no great significance for tradition history, his Ch. V (pp. 168-259), in which he deals with the "Problem of the Pentateuch" and with the Deuteronomistic and Chronistic Histories, certainly is. The author begins with a critical review of Pentateuchal research before and after Wellhausen, and ends on a reference to the final collapse of the Wellhausen era. Here he marshalls the troops of the opposition, a group composed of fundamentalists, Jews, conservative exegetes and orientalists. Johs. Pedersen's contribution is singled out as especially creative and Nyberg's use of oral tradition is represented as thoroughly consistent tradition history. After this, Engnell personally attacks the criteria of source criticism: doublets, repetitions, contradictions, stylistic peculiarities, "constants", and the criterion of the Divine Name. This broadside is followed by the author's own "positive account" of tradition history, which assumes the following two theses: (1) that the traditional materials of the Pentateuch are generally very old, and that (2) their redaction took place quite late[3]. Engnell's third thesis parallels that of Noth, in that he also affirms (3) the division between Gen-Num, held to be without traces of Deuteronomistic activity, and Deut, which forms the introduction to the Deuteronomistic Historical Work.

By Engnell's account, Noth holds that P is the literary foundation into which J and E have been integrated, while according to his own view P was the last tradent and "publisher" of these materials. Whether this distinction is hairsplitting or reflects substantive differences is difficult to determine, but it may well be this problem we again encounter later on if we compare Noth's or R. Smend's opinion with that of R. Rendtorff, who now clearly tends to regard P as a redactional and interpretative stratum (Smend 1978, pp. 47-59; Rendtorff 1977).

Engnell characterizes his fourth thesis as posing the most pressing task of tradition history, not the banal observation that it is necessary to distinguish between legal and narrative materials, but (4) *to reveal the shorter units and special blocks of tradition* (1945, p. 213). Exactly what is meant by this is debatable, though Engnell can hardly be thinking of individual stories, since these, of course, are the objects of form-critical study. In the following pages it appears that by "shorter units" Engnell in fact has in mind such large complexes as the Joseph Novelle, the Abraham narratives, the Primeval History, migration legends, legal collections, the Passover legend, the Sinai tradition and the Balaam narrative. The task of the scholar is said not to consist in analyzing these short (actually: large) units by literary-critical or historical means, but in reading them as they stand in their de-cultified, historicized form.

Here Ringgren's observations are quite correct, that Engnell's version of tradition history actually consists in stopping at the final result, that is, at the finished literary product; and furthermore, that Engnell's concentration on one particular concern nevertheless always forced him to analyze the development of the tradition (Ringgren 1966, col. 646). This was his concern to discover the cultic-ritual pattern held to underlie the text in question: sacral kingship, the king as the guarantor of fertility, the sacred marriage (*hieros gamos*), the Tammuz-like character of the king, his ritual suffering or humiliation. Thus Ringgren also rightly notes that in reality Engnell's tradition history has to do with *religio-historical Motiv-analyse*.

Emphasis on the finished literary product, the composition as it stands, as the primary datum of research, runs the risk of neglecting the "historical" in tradition history, a point many of Engnell's critics have also stressed. This ultimately leads to the study of redaction history, compositional technique and structuralism; and, as Ringgren has further pointed out, it is in this direction that Agge Carlson, one of Engnell's more prominent students, has in fact concentrated his activities. Since Carlson's subject-matter lies primarily outside of the Pentateuch I shall not discuss his work more extensively here but con-

fine my remarks to his contribution to the Festschrift for Ringgren
dealing with the P-prologue in Gen 1:2 - 2:3 (Carlson 1977). According to Carlson, this complex contains elements which anticipate central themes in the P-Work and more or less unify it; this applies, for
example, to the command to man to be fruitful and multiply, which is
repeated to Noah, Abraham and the other patriarchs, and is reflected
in the growth of the Israelite population in Egypt in Exod 1: 7. It is
also developed in the Toledoth chain, where Carlson sees 2: 4 (both a
and b) as a superscription to Genesis 2 - 4, and he accordingly regards
P as the last tradent, rather than an independent source.

Because of the demands on Engnell's time levied by the task of
publishing *SBU* (a new edition appeared in 1962-63) and an extensive
teaching schedule in both Uppsala and Stockholm, he never managed
to publish a detailed traditio-historical monograph. Moreover, while
Engnell's publications in *SBU* were independent scholarly work and
were both lucid and readable, they were perhaps slightly too much *ex
cathedra*, characterized as they were by presuppositions which were already fully developed in 1945.

In the world outside of Scandinavia, Engnell became known mainly
through second-hand accounts and in polemical articles. It was therefore a welcome event when, after his death, a selection of his articles
in *SBU* were translated into English and published in both the USA
and England (Engnell 1969). As is well known, the whole field of traditio-historical research has recently been surveyed by Douglas A.
Knight (1973); Knight devotes 31 pages to Engnell, and the chapter is,
in full justice to the facts, entitled, "Ivan Engnell: The Center of the
Debate"[4].

Since Engnell

In the following pages it will not be possible to provide an exhaustive
survey of traditio-historical efforts in modern Pentateuch criticism,
neither as far as Scandinavia nor the ambit of European-American-Ja-
panese research is concerned. Instead, I shall attempt to point to some
of the problems scholars have been concerned with and to some tendencies evident in the last forty years of study (cf. Grønbæk 1972).

a) As is well known, *source-critical analysis* owes its origins to the
Book of Genesis, and, additionally, J. Astruc's major observation was
that in Genesis Moses recounted things he had not himself experien-

ced and must therefore have been dependent on written materials. To this very day Genesis remains the text corpus to which the Documentary Hypothesis seems to be the most appropriate, whereas generations of exegetes have experienced the *difficulties* involved in attempting to transfer the J, E and P of Genesis to Exod-Num, even if Exod chs. 3 and 6 *may* be able to provide some support for the notion of an Elohistic and a Priestly source. Moreover, considering the way tradition historians now pose the question of the development of the Pentateuch, it becomes even more problematical to attempt to apply the Genesis sources to all of the narrative materials in Exod and Num, comprised as they are of Exodus legends, the Sinai pericope, migration legends and the Balaam story. The reason is that for historians of tradition Genesis is simply no longer the point of departure, since the emphasis has shifted to Exod 1-15. This innovation was inaugurated by Johs. Pedersen (1934a, pp. 545-551; Eng. pp. 728-737; 1934b.) and taken up by both von Rad and Noth, who, however, did not draw the same consequence as Pedersen with respect to the value of source criticism. One would have thought that the insight of tradition history would here have tempted scholars to begin their literary-critical analysis of Exod 1-15 — very much as the texts themselves seem to require — *without reference to the "sources" in Genesis*, and only afterwards to enquire as to possible wider literary connexions once the materials in Exod-Num had been thoroughly analyzed.

b) Another problem is presented by *form criticism*, which is primarily concerned with the smallest literary units, such as individual myths, sagas, legends, etiologies, lists, tribal songs, and so forth. What are we to say if the methodological requirements of source criticism entail that we separate such passages as Gen 15:1-6 and 7-21, which are promises of offspring and land, respectively? Or, to put the matter another way, is literary criticism always to receive a higher priority than form criticism?

c) A third problem concerns *the dating of the traditional materials and the sources*. The respect von Rad and Noth commanded even in circles which were quite far from their homeland ensured a sort of consensus on an early date for the oldest Pentateuchal source. Von Rad advocated, as mentioned above, Solomon's "freigeistige Ära" in the case of J, while Noth pushed the date even further back with his hypothetical common G-Grundlage. Noth held that whether "G" was oral or written, it will have preceded J and E, though its structure will have resembled J's, and that it could be dated to pre-monarchical times (Noth 1948, p. 48)[5].

However, if these works were formed around the time of the introduction of the Monarchy or shortly thereafter, and if their purpose was, among other things, to legitimate the possession of the land by the Israelite tribes and ideologically to underwrite their claims to power, a major difficulty arises. This is, why do we hear nothing, or practically nothing, about Sinai, Moses and the Exodus, Abraham, Isaac and Jacob in the *individual traditions employed by Dtr in his History*, in the *pre-exilic Psalms*, or in the *pre-exilic prophets*? Hosea, of course, is an exception, but the fact that he was the only North Israelite among the prophets partially weakens his value as evidence. Furthermore, if one maintains that J was not only a collector but also a reworker of traditions, author and theologian, then it becomes difficult to insist on so early a date as von Rad's. Consider, for example, the fact that in two of the texts which, according to von Rad, are closest to J, namely Gen 12:1-3 and Gen 24, we find respectively not only a programme asserting Israel's universal significance which is reminiscent of Deutero-Isaiah, but also a well-developed concept of Divine Providence coupled with a conscious insistence on segregation from the inhabitants of Canaan. That is to say, we find a programme which might seem to have much in common with Deuteronomic-Deuteronomistic tendencies.

d) A fourth problem concerns the *relationship between narrative texts and legal materials*. No one has ever really successfully demonstrated any *necessary* connexion between the oldest sources and the (presumably) oldest legal complexes: the Book of the Covenant, the Decalogue and the so-called "ritual Decalogue" (in Exod 34). Furthermore, even if one took Exod 20 in a slightly older form (!), plus Exod 21-23 together with an E source, and Exod 34 together with a J source, one would nevertheless be left with the impression of two narrative sources in which the legal materials played an astonishingly small part (cf. E. Nielsen 1982). It is quite different with D, in which the apparently most ancient materials are purely legal, though dependent on and in part further developments of materials in the Book of the Covenant. Here the narrative elements almost certainly reflect nascent Deuteronomistic activity.

As far as P is concerned it is clear that with the exception of the Creation, the Flood and the covenant with Abraham[6] the narratives are a thin line connected to the Toledoth idea. Further, the Exodus bits practically function as additions to and continuations of the pre-Priestly basic narratives. And finally, even P's share in the authorship of the account of Moses' death is difficult to determine. Ranged a-gainst these meager materials is a massive body of legislation containing great blocks of laws (on the Tabernacle, Exod 25-31; on sacrifice, Lev 1-7; on priests, Lev 8-10; on purity and impurity, Lev 11-15; on the great Day of Atonement, Lev 16; on the festivals, Num 28f.). In order to redeem P as a real parallel source to J and E, Noth resolutely excised *all* of the legal matter in it. But why on earth would a P narrator recounting the story of the Flood refrain from distinguishing between clean and unclean animals, or from mentioning Noah's sacrifice? Similarly, P never mentions the sacrifices of the Patriarchs. All of this makes sense only if P *later on* proclaims divine guidance with respect to sacrifices and to the distinction between pure and impure, and between clean and unclean animals. For both D and P one can hardly avoid the conclusion of a necessary relation between the narratives and the legal materials[7]. As far as the pre-Deuteronomistic narratives are concerned there is a slight connexion provided by the fact that an altar law in Exod 20:24-26 is situated before the Book of the Covenant, and that this law, which is somewhat retouched in its present form, accords reasonably well with the many narratives dealing with sanctuaries in Josh-2 Kgs, and to the patriarchal accounts of JE.

e) Finally, we may mention as a fifth problem *the legal material itself*, inviting as it is to both form-critical and traditio-historical treatment. The Decalogue and its relationship to D is a special problem in its own right: the formulation of the first four or five Commandments seems to be redolent of Deuteronomic ideas, and yet Exod 20, which in its present form is assigned to P, seems to represent an older form of the Decalogue than Deut 5. This leads in turn to the question of the precise relationship between D and P, including, again, the question of dates.

Recent Developments

This catalogue of problems could doubtless be extended indefinitely, but I should instead prefer to mention some recent developments in the treatment of the Pentateuch in order subsequently to conclude on a discussion of two important contributions to the problem of the Pentateuch by H.H. Schmid and Rolf Rendtorff, respectively.

A *conservative* tendency has been in evidence; it seeks to find an authentic historical (Mosaic) nucleus among the materials and has chosen the Decalogue as its object, much as we might expect, which it has attempted to illuminate with the aid of Hittite vassal treaties. G.E. Mendenhall opened this line of enquiry with a couple of articles (1954 a and b); he was swiftly seconded by K. Baltzer's monograph, *Das Bundesformular* (1960). In brief, the Hittite monarch's presentation of himself, his good deeds towards his vassals, his fundamental demands and more detailed stipulations concerning the treaty, plus practical rules ensuring the preservation and regular public reading of the treaty's text have been compared with the Decalogue, the narrative of the two tablets, the covenant at the foot of Sinai (Exod 24: 3-8), and the preservation of the tablets in the Ark. The theory has been sympathetically reviewed by Kapelrud (1964), who feels that the sojourn of the Exodus-tribes in the oasis of Kadesh prior to the entry into the land virtually requires something like the Decalogue as its instrument of unification. The Covenant will thus have originated in Kadesh: it was there the Decalogue received its *Urform*. I personally expressed serious reservations as to this line of research in my analysis of the Decalogue (1965), and a few years later Lothar Perlitt (1969) pulled the rug out from under the feet of the adherents of Mendenhall's thesis, who were quite numerous in 1969[8].

The conservative impulse has also come to expression in a wide-ranging project by Sven Tengström called *Die Hexateucherzählung. Eine literaturgeschichtliche Studie* (1976). If in company with Engnell, one understands "tradition history" to be synonymous with "oral tradition", then Tengström's study is *not* traditio-historical, since he both embraces the possibility of early literary activity – early, that is to say, before the establishment of the Monarchy – and methodologically proceeds by literary-critical means, although apparently unencumbered by the four-source hypothesis. Tengström concludes by arriving at the approximate text of a *Grundschrift* running from the beginning of the Abraham narratives and ending on the account of the covenant of the tribes at Shechem in Josh 24. Tengström's project invites respect; it is carried out with impressive consistency, and its result is perhaps only a shade more conservative than Noth's "G", which was held to underlie J and E and to date from the pre-monarchical period.

Tengström has only very recently followed his first work up with a book entitled *Die Toledotformel* (1982). I should like on this occasion to thank him for making me a present of it, and to say that while I would take exception to some details in the work, I think his main thesis is entirely correct: an analysis of the *toledoth* formula in P shows P to have been more a reworker, expander and interpreter of older materials than an independent source. Here Tengström is in full agreement with Rolf Rendtorff and other recent researchers. Similarly, in his analysis of, among other things, the occurrence of the first *toledoth* formula i Gen 2: 4, Tengström is on the same wavelength as the above-mentioned article by Agge Carlson, in the Ringgren-Festschrift, although curiously enough Carlson's article does not figure in either Tengström's notes or his bibliography.

The somewhat *radical* impulse which Perlitt's book has opened the floodgates for in German research, but which in reality was long pursued by both Pedersen and Engnell, has left its mark on Heike Friis' article on the Exile and the Israelite understanding of history (1975). Using comparative material from Egypt and Babylon in the 7th-6th centuries, Friis shows that the period around the exile of Israel and Judah was characterized by retrospective historical interests, by emphasis on the significance of cult and ritual, and by a conscious effort to exclude foreign influences. Similar tendencies are evident in the Deuteronomic and Deuteronomistic literatures, as well as in the present form of the patriarchal narratives, which so frequently reiterate the theme of the people's right to the land. Friis further demonstrates the presence of this Tendenz in the patriarchal stories by analysis of the narratives about the "threat to the ancestress" (Gen 12; 20; 26). The structure of these accounts reveals oddly common features with the Joseph Novella and the story of Moses: exile, reasonably secure circumstances, peril, punishment, humiliation, salvation and reward, all of which are summed up by the following moral: retain your identity during your banishment; God will reward you for it and lead you home.

I am inclined to think that Friis' article over-interprets the facts to some extent, and for other reasons I should prefer to see the period after the collapse of the Northern Kingdom as the era when Israelite and Judaean tra itions were combined. This will have been the time when the Deuteronomic movement, sustained by historical circles from North Israel, won influence with the Judaeans, when the North Israelite Moses and Exodus traditions achieved decisive importance, and the circles ultimately responsible for the Priestly Writing began to gain ground. This would realize Pedersen's pronouncement that, "The more the self-confidence of the people was shaken, the more it clung to its history." Moreover, in a way it would also correspond to H.S. Nyberg's dictum that the written, literary recording of the traditions was related to a general crisis of confidence, and just such a crisis will have occurred with the rise of the Assyrian empire around the middle of the 8th century.

H. H. Schmid and Rolf Rendtorff

The very critical attitude towards the four-source hypothesis which has characterized some traditio-historical research, taken together with the tendency to date the oldest traditions quite late, has, apparently independently of Scandinavian research, received a degree of support from two of the younger Germanic scholars, the Swiss H.H. Schmid (1976) and the German Rolf Rendtorff (1977).

Schmid does not begin with Genesis, but with Exodus: Moses' call, the plagues, the crossing of the Reed Sea, examples from the wandering in the desert and the Sinai pericope; only subsequently does he discuss the patriarchal narratives in Genesis. Schmid's criticism is "system-immanent", i.e., he starts from the classical source-critical position, and his attack has not so much to do with the division of sources as with the by now time-honoured dating of J to the time of Solomon. Schmid points out that the call of Moses is formulated in a manner reminiscent of the prophetic call narratives[9], and that the plague stories are recounted more or less according to the scheme employed by Dtr in the Book of Judges. Finally, he holds that the fraction of Exod 14 which is normally assigned to J (vv. 13f and 31), which includes the injunction to the people not to fear but to remain quiet and believe, is typologically dependent on the royal salvation oracle, though appearing here in democratized form. H.H. Schmid's perhaps arbitrarily chosen examples from Exod 15 and 17 and Num 11 and 21 display a Tendenz analogous to the Deuteronomic-Deuteronomistic philosophy of history. As he further points out, as far as the

Sinai traditions are concerned, it is in the first place debatable how much or little can be attributed to the Yahwist. In the second place, the Sinai traditions as such derive from a northern provenance (Judg 5; Ps 68), and are not connected with any notion of a covenant, which of course according to Perlitt was a late-blooming idea in any case. In all of these J materials, according to Schmid, there is nothing to be found which argues for a Solomonic provenance, and much that argues against it. Like Rendtorff[10], Schmid examines the promises to the patriarchs concerning numerous offspring (which he holds must be secondary to narratives relating the promise of a son), concerning blessing (which must be secondary to the blessing itself), and concerning the possession of the land which in Schmid's view presupposes an era when possession of the land was in jeopardy, i.e., the age of Dtn.

The author mentions that while J was seen as a collector by Gunkel, who also considered the promises about the land to be secondary, to von Rad they were the heart and soul of the Yahwistic theologian's literary and theological endeavour. Schmid's subsequent traditio-historical considerations lead to an evaluation of the Sinai covenant tradition as late, and the Exodus tradition as North Israelite, which he supports by an examination of the four prophets of the 8th century. Thus the connexion between the Exodus and Sinai traditions, which, apart from JE, is first demonstrable in Deuteronomistic and post-exilic literature, cannot be assigned to Noth's "G" from the period of the Judges, or to von Rad's "J" from the Solomonic era. As far as Moses is concerned, the only real reference to him among the pre-exilic prophets is in Hos 12:14.

Finally, there are the promises to the patriarchs, whose presupposition is held to be the united Israel. However, since Noth's amphictyony thesis has collapsed, the promises can not be held to be pre-Davidic; and since even the historical traditions of the Davidic-Solomonic era do not suggest a living and active concept of a united Israel, the patriarchal stories cannot be derived from the Israelite empire. We must again seek recourse to the Deuteronomic-Deuteronomistic age.

H.H. Schmid concludes his provocative book with a series of open questions:
1) concerning the relationships obtaining among the Yahwistic, proto-Deuteronomic, Deuteronomic and Deuteronomistic traditions;
2) concerning the theological and literary connexions between the various themes of the Pentateuch;

3) concerning the relationship between literary criticism as a method and source-division as a hypothesis; and
4) concerning the relationship between literary and form criticism. Is W. Richter, among others, right in asserting that literary-critical analysis must always precede form-critical analysis?
Schmid's own conclusion on the subject of J is that the stratum is closely related to Dt-Dtr. J is characterized by a philosophy of history, and a philosophy of history is held necessarily to be a late product arising from the great crisis of Israel's history, and dependent on the prophetic literature.

In his address to the recent conference in Vienna, H.H. Schmid stressed that new perspectives are necessary, now that Noth's amphictyony theory and von Rad's dating of the short historical Credo are no longer viable, and now that scholars have realized that Judah did not belong to Israel. One doubts whether Schmid's address really contains all that many new perspectives, but he does at all events energetically urge that we should not isolate Pentateuchal criticism from the study of the rest of Old Testament literature, and remarks in this connexion: "Ein halbes Buch über die Überlieferungsgeschichte zu schreiben, ohne je einen Blick auf das übrige Alte Testament zu werfen, kann daher m.E. nur aus Zufall das Richtige treffen."(1981, p.394).

One wonders whether this last remark does not refer to Rolf Rendtorff's *Das überlieferungsgeschichtliche Problem des Pentateuch* of whose four chapters the second and longest deals with "Die Vätergeschichten als Beispiel einer 'grösseren Einheit' im Rahmen des Pentateuch" (1977, pp.28-79). First I ought perhaps to mention that Rolf Rendtorff is a friend of Scandinavia; he often vacations in Denmark and has lectured during the Exegetical Day at Uppsala in 1965 on literary criticism and tradition history (Rendtorff 1966). Already at that time Rendtorff displayed considerable openness, and although he also expressed some criticism of tradition history in Scandinavia, he was interested in building bridges, removing obstacles to common understanding, and so forth. Back in 1965 Rendtorff still affirmed the source hypothesis, i.e., the parallelism of P and J, but since then form-critical and traditio-historical studies have led him to a virtual showdown with the four-source hypothesis. This process began with Rendtorff's address to the Edinburgh conference at which he declared the programme to which he has since adhered, especially in *Das überliefer-*

ungsgeschichtliche Problem des Pentateuch. At the Edinburgh conference, Rendtorff spoke of the dilemma of Pentateuchal criticism,
which he saw as consisting in the fact that the documentary hypothesis presupposes authors behind the sources, while literary studies since
the time of Gunkel (including form-critical and saga research) have instead tended to describe the so-called "sources" as collections of
blocks of tradition. Thus the passages in which the collector's own
profile could conceivably be expressed have become smaller and smaller; for example, in the case of Noth's J, this is restricted to Gen 12:1-
3. Furthermore, says Rendtorff, if we examine the promises to the patriarchs in Genesis in order to broaden our insight into J's theology,
we discover, first, that this "theology" only applies to J's share of the
patriarchal narratives, and not the Moses traditions; and, second, that
there is not just one layer of promises in Genesis, but layer upon
layer.

As I have mentioned, all this is more closely argued in Rendtorff's
book from 1977. The author here proposes that we examine the larger units of material in isolation without committing ourselves in advance to notions about continuous documentary sources running
throughout the entire Pentateuch. Such units would include the patriarchal narratives; the Exodus legend in Exod 1-14; Israel in the desert,
Exod 16-18, Num 11-20; and the Sinai traditions, Exod 19-24 and 32-
34. The Sinai account is extremely independent in relation to the
Exodus motif, and the occasional references in the desert tradition to
Egypt only serve to establish contrast but contain no recollections of
or connexions with the principal motif of Exod 1-14. Should we enquire whether there are any connective elements among the J materials of the Pentateuch, Rendtorff answers, "yes indeed"! Such connexions are to be found in Yahweh's sworn assurances to the fathers
concerning the land (Gen 50:24; 26:3; 24:7; 22:16; and in Exod 13:5.
11 and 33:1-3; finally, in Num 11:11-25 and 32:11); but these are not
fully integrated into their contexts; they always exude a certain air of
being secondary additions, and they are intimately related to Deut. In
fact, these connexions are closer to D than to J! Thus Rendtorff arrives at the following conclusions:

1) There *is* no Yahwist responsible for both the narratives of the patriarchs and the other epic materials in the Pentateuch.

2) It is first Deuteronomy-like or Deuteronomically-coloured strata,
expressed in Yahweh's oath to the patriarchs, which have the function

of assembling large and originally independent units into a unified Pentateuch.

3) As far as P is concerned, Rendtorff asserts that it is not a continuous narrative, but only one or more layers of redaction.

Rendtorff's attitude towards literary criticism is that it is certainly necessary, but ought not to be burdened by the four-source hypothesis. Further, a theory about sources can only be accepted if, after thorough traditio-historical analysis of all parts of the Pentateuch has been carried out, such a theory proves to offer the most obvious explanation of the origin of the present text. Thus Rendtorff's slogan is, "Abkehr von der Urkundenhypothese."

I shall stop here, but my satisfaction with these two new initiatives from Germanic scholars is mixed with one regret: the only Scandinavian work mentioned by H.H. Schmid is my own little book on the Ten Commandments; otherwise he refers only to an article by Magnus Ottosson and a lecture by A. Lauha. The rest is German, German, German. Rendtorff is only slightly better in this respect, but of Johs. Pedersen's production he refers only to "Passahlegende" (ZAW 1934), and to *Israel* I-IV not at all. Oh dear, who would have thought that Germany could be so provincial?

REMARKS OF AN OUTSIDER CONCERNING SCANDINAVIAN TRADITION HISTORY WITH EMPHASIS ON THE DAVIDIC TRADITIONS

Timo Veijola

Introduction: the Programme of Ivan Engnell

Whoever seeks to evaluate Scandinavian traditio-historical research is first obliged to define what he understands to be tradition history. Scandinavian tradition history could not be considered an independent branch of study without reference to the name of Ivan Engnell. Admittedly, Engnell adknowledged his indebtedness for a number of important impulses to earlier scholars, both in Scandinavia (above all H.S. Nyberg and Johs. Pedersen) and in Great Britain (J.E. James, A.M. Hocart, and the entire "myth and ritual school"; Engnell 1945, p. 40)[1]. However, without Engnell's personal contribution an "Uppsala Circle" or "Scandinavian School"[2] would hardly have existed as an independent entity within the field of OT studies, even though he personally opposed any kind of school-formation and regarded such a tendency as a threat to academic freedom (Engnell 1960, p. 14)[3].

The more general characteristics of the method [4] founded by Engnell are well known in Scandinavia, and I shall accordingly be brief in my remarks about them. Of signal importance for Engnell's understanding of the world of the Old Testament was the hypothesis of the importance of oral tradition in the Old Testament which he derived from his teacher, H.S. Nyberg (Engnell 1945, pp.39-44)[5]. This emphasis entailed by the same token a devaluation of the importance attached to the written tradition, which was held to be for the most part a product of exilic or, more probably, post-exilic Judaism (1945, pp.29-

29

43). Thus Engnell ceaselessly stressed the reliability of the oral tradition, to which, in his view, the cultic-sacral character of the Old Testament traditions had also contributed. Moreover, Engnell affirmed that the written fixation of these materials constituted no significant incident during the process of tradition (1945, pp.29.42)[6]. In addition to this fundamental stance, Engnell also evinced a methodologically extremely conservative attitude towards the MT, which allowed only scant significance to the Versions (1945, pp.28-34)[7], a view already previously adumbrated in Nyberg's *Studien zum Hoseabuche* (1935). Furthermore, Engnell's advocacy of oral tradition led him into a passionate conflict with literary criticism, which he did not regard as a method, but as a school embodied in the person of J. Wellhausen (Engnell 1969, p. 10). Nor could Engnell resist asserting that the literary-critical enterprise was an anachronistic *interpretatio europeica moderna* (1960, pp. 17.21; 1969, p. 53), which, also in the form represented by Wellhausen, was dependent on an untenably evolutionistic understanding of history (1945, pp. 10.175). Although Engnell subsequently retreated from his onesided emphasis on oral tradition as a result of the criticisms of G. Widengren — above all 1948 and 1959 — and others, and was able to accept the notion of parallel oral and literary traditions (1960, p. 23; 1969, pp. 7.65), his negative attitude towards literary criticism remained strangely constant. In contradistinction to his Norwegian colleague, S. Mowinckel[8], Engnell found himself unable to compromise and remarked polemically in 1960 that "the break with the literary-critical method must be radical; no compromise is possible. The old method must be replaced by a new one" (1960, p. 21).

By a new, alternative method Engnell of course meant none other than the traditio-historical approach inaugurated by himself and which, according to him, and in contradistinction to literary criticism, was founded upon a "realistic" understanding of the Bible (1969, p. 11). To Engnell, traditio-historical criticism was namely not merely one method among others, but simply *the* method; thus, although it contained a variety of facets it represented in the last analysis the only correct approach to the study of the Old Testament (1960, pp. 18.21. 28)[9].

Among the proponents of the earlier forms of tradition history Engnell recognized the contributions of the fathers of form criticism, H. Gunkel and H. Gressmann, as well as those of M. Noth and S. Mowinckel, although in his eyes these figures had all been enthralled by the now dated fundamentally literary approach, and he accordingly held their results to be in need of correction (Engnell 1969, pp. 3f).

Engnell described his own traditio-historical method as both analytic and synthetic. He understood analysis to require above all both the formal and compositional analysis of short units and stressed the importance of observing the role played by the various compositional techniques. Nor was analysis felt to be limited to purely formal characteristics; it also included considerations of content. Matters of literary, historical, ideological, psychological, sociological, archeological, and culture-historical significance were included as well. The second phase was that of synthesis, which entailed the interpretation of the short units in relation to their context and corresponds to the goal of contemporary redactio-historical study (1960, pp. 22f; 1969, pp. 4f)[10].

A noteworthy characteristic of Engnell's description of his method is that it was not held to be neutral with regard to content; rather, in the analytical phase it was closely attached to the views of the "myth and ritual school". This opened the door to "patternism", which Engnell termed in at least one passage "the only correct method" (1969, p. 26)[11]. Patternism presupposes the existence of a comprehensive cultic scheme which was thought to have been present in various forms throughout the ancient Orient. As is well known, its most important element consisted of the role of the divine king who suffered during the New Year Festival in battle with the forces of chaos; here he was provisionally vanquished, after which he (superficially) died and descended into Sheol, for ultimately to resurrect, accede to the throne, perform a *hieros gamos*, and "determine the destinies", i.e., ensure fertility and blessing for the coming year (1969, p. 182)[12]. All of this was held to have been performed by the king in his capacity as *deus incarnatus*. Although Engnell emphasized that this scheme could not be used as a sort of universal passkey, he did not doubt its existence in ancient Israel (1969, pp. 23-26).

Another characteristic aspect of Engnell's description of traditio-historical method is his emphasis on "ideological" analysis. This emphasis is indicated by the frequency of occurrence of the words "idea, ideology, ideological" in Engnell's works[13]. These terms have also been assimilated by his school[14]. This is in marked contrast to the extremely rare mention of "theology" by Engnell, and one is tempted to suppose that for Engnell "ideology" has replaced "theology". On the other hand, it would be incorrect to maintain that Engnell had no grasp of the "theological" meaning of the texts; rather, he stipulated that the ultimate goal of the Old Testament scholar was to study the religious contents of the Old Testament on their own terms, and in furtherance of this assertion he criticized the literary critics for having to a large extent neglected the religious content of the Old Testament (1945, pp. 8f). While Engnell never expressly ruled out the possibility of composing a scientifically responsible Old Testament theology, he firmly insisted that such a study be carried out "in a purely historical way" (1960, p. 30). Since this ideal could scarcely be realized except in the form of an account of the history of Old Testament religion, one is inclined to wonder whether this opinion of Engnell's does not explain why Old Testament theology has merited no serious attention whatsoever in the Scandinavian research of the last decades.

The ultimate impression the reader is left with after perusal of Engnell's writings is the feeling that Engnell's tradition history was an ambitious programme which was intuitively adumbrated by the author but never effectuated in detail. This is completely clear in *Studies in Divine Kingship in the Ancient Near East* (1943), in which the consequences of the work for the study of the Old Testament are sketched in a research programme of only four pages (pp. 174-177). Even less could one claim of the "traditio-historical introduction" to Engnell's *Gamla Testamentet* I (1945) that it succeeds in realizing the author's programme. Rather, it, too, merely contains an account of the method and of the principles according to which work is to be performed. The actual demonstration was to have appeared in the second volume, which, however, was never published, although it partially exists in proof-sheets[15]. Was it external or internal events that prevented the completion of this work?

Because of the both fragmentary and programmatic nature of Engnell's initiative, great expectations have naturally accrued to his pupils, to whom the task has fallen of demonstrating their master's thesis through the investigation of the pertinent texts. But before I proceed to the question of the further development and testing of Engnell's theses with respect to a particular theme, it will be necessary first to account for their reception in non-Scandinavian Old Testament circles.

The predominantly negative reaction to Engnell's ideas on the Continent and above all in the German language area should be both well known and in need of no further demonstration. The names of M. Noth (1950) and K.-H. Bernhardt (1961) may serve as examples of the reaction to Engnell in West and East Germany, respectively. The Finnish position vis à vis Engnell's programme will, however, be less well known. Shortly after the publication of *Gamla Testamentet* three distinguished Finnish scholars, R. Gyllenberg, A.F. Puukko, and A. Lauha, recorded their reactions to Engnell's work. Gyllenberg's review (1946) is basically favourably disposed towards Engnell; among other things he welcomes Engnell's conservative text-critical principles as "good" and "sound", and refers further in this connexion to the insignificant part played by textual emendation in New Testament scholarship (Gyllenberg 1946, p. 157). However, Gyllenberg is not wholly satisfied with the new traditio-historical research; he finds that, despite its name, it is marked by "a certain degree of time-less-ness" and requires to be corrected by a *historical* point of view (p. 158). But it is Engnell's treatment of Pentateuchal criticism that most disturbs Gyllenberg; here he is principally exercised by the role accorded by Engnell to the oral tradition and he detects an inconsistency in the fact that at one point Engnell assigns the written fixation of the Pentateuch to the Exilic or Post-exilic period, while at another he regards Israelite literature as the last development of Canaanite literature. Personally, Gyllenberg held it to be likely that a not-insignificant portion of the Old Testament traditions had achieved written fixation already considerably earlier than the Exile (p. 159).

The Old Testament scholar A.F. Puukko is more critical in his evaluation of Engnell and visibly irritated by the self-assurance with which the latter advances his views, as well as by the fact that he completely ignores Puukko's major work from 1910, *Das Deuteronomium* (1947, p. 66). Puukko's main reaction is to defend Wellhausen and the literary-critical method, which he feels can not be dismissed as easily as Engnell believes (pp. 64-68). While not outright rejecting the significance of oral tradition for the understanding of Old Testament narratives, Puukko nevertheless points out that we do not in fact know these oral traditions. If the doublets, obscurities, and tensions in the texts are to be explained by oral tradition, says Puukko, this in reality means only "that one now transfers the unknown with which one works considerably farther back in time, with the result that the scholar's imagination has even more room to manoeuvre than previously" (p. 70) — a remark that is surely not completely unfounded.

The third and youngest of Engnell's then-contemporary Finnish critics, A. Lauha (1947a), follows the tracks of his teacher Puukko in his review of *Gamla Testamentet*. Thus he regards favourably Engnell's emphasis on circles of tradition while characterizing the role of oral tradition in Engnell's scheme as an hypothesis which is disproved by mere archeological evidence, e.g. Ras Shamra (p. 61). Lauha further considers the question of sacral kingship ideology and concludes that the historical texts of the Old Testament evince no knowledge of it (p. 62); this critique is more extensively presented in Lauha's article (1947b). Here he asserts that the currency of royal ideologies in other cultures of the ancient Near East can not justify our using the notion as a universal key to all of the Old Testament texts. Lauha does not deny the presence of sporadic traces of a royal ideology in the Old Testament, but sees them as no more than occasional survivals of Canaanite influences which are in no way representative of the Old Testament attitude towards monarchy (1947b, p. 184). Further, Lauha explains the metaphors applied to the king in Ps 2, 110, and 2 Sam 7:14 as due to the influence of a court style which does not reflect the central tenets of the Yahwistic faith. Were the opposite the case, as he points out, we should expect the royal ideology also to have left its mark on the historical texts, which, according to Engnell himself, very faithfully preserve the original views (p. 186). But this is in no way the case; rather, from its inception the Monarchy was represented as an empirico-historical phenomenon, and furthermore, in addition to it there were in Israel circles which opposed the Monarchy for religious or social reasons (Jdg 8:23; 9:8ff; 1 Sam 8:7f) (p. 187).

Nor does Lauha accept the explanation that the anti-monarchical sentiment is to be traced to priestly circles, since this explanation contradicts the postulate according to which the royal ideology was at home in the cult: "the priests who opposed sacral kingship would probably not have accorded an important position in the cult they themselves led to an ideology to which they were opposed" (p. 188). Lauha's criticism of the royal ideology is noteworthy in that it essentially anticipates by three years the objections voiced by M. Noth in his methodological disquisition (1950), which reached a wider public.

Briefly to summarize Finnish reactions to Engnell's traditio-historical method, it seems that they were in the main dismissive, and the passage of time has made no important changes in this picture. Thus

if one is today still predisposed to speak of a "Scandinavian school"
– so expessly Nyberg 1972, p. 10 – one should observe the caution
that in its strict and most literal sense the adjective "Scandinavian"
is not to be taken to apply to Finland. Seen in this light, it is appropriate for a Finn to discuss as an "outsider" the practice of tradition history in Scandinavia.

The Traditions about David as Viewed by Scandinavian Historians of Tradition

Although Scandinavian traditio-historical research owed its beginnings
to the inspiring research initiatives of I. Engnell, it would be both anachronistic and unfair to judge this branch of study on the basis of his
works alone. Of equal importance to Engnell's programme are the further developments to which his ideas were subjected by the Scandinavian school. It is my intention in what follows to use the example of
the Davidic traditions to indicate how the principles and theses established by Engnell have been preserved in further research.

To Engnell David was no subordinate personality, but obviously
the most important figure in the entire Old Testament, since it was
David who, according to Engnell, brought about the great syncretism
between Canaanite and Israelite religion. Tendencies in this direction
were held to have been present even earlier, since already Saul's kingship had sacral characteristics (Engnell 1962-63 I, col. 404), but these
tendencies will first have borne fruit when Jerusalem was taken and
full symbiosus was established between the Canaanite El Elyon and
Israelite Yahweh (1945, pp. 119. 138. 145)[16]. The Canaanite divinity El Elyon will then subsequently have been worshipped in Jerusalem
in the form of Yahweh. The most striking expression of this worship
was the sacral role of the king, which culminated in the ritual of the
New Year Festival (1969, pp. 36. 41. 223)[17].

Thus, if we take account of the fact that for Engnell sacral kingship
was the central theme of Israelite religion (1943, p. 175; 1945, p.
144), and that he linked this theme directly to the concept of Messia-
nism (1943, p. 176)[18], then it is no exaggeration to claim that for
Engnell David's role in the history of Israelite religion was second to
none. However, here it is necessary to recall that to Engnell "David"

was not a proper name but a regnal title which the historical David will have adopted from the Jebusites after the capture of Jerusalem (1943, p. 176; 1969, p. 83). Etymologically speaking, Engnell derived the title from the Canaanite fertility divinity, *Dōd*. Furthermore, Engnell understood the psalmic superscription *ledāwīd* as applying to those of the royal psalms which had played a part in the New Year Festival in connexion with sacral kingship (1943, pp. 176f)[19]. Engnell did not question the authenticity of most of the psalm superscriptions.

Since Engnell's day, four comprehensive monographs on the Davidic traditions have appeared in Scandinavia: G.W. Ahlström's dissertation, *Psalm 89* (1959), R.A. Carlson's dissertation on the Second Book of Samuel, *David, the Chosen King* (1964), J.H. Grønbæk's dissertation, *Die Geschichte vom Aufstieg Davids* (1971), and T.N.D. Mettinger's comprehensive monograph, *King and Messiah* (1976), which deals with the civil and sacral legitimation of Israelite kings in the light of the traditions describing the early monarchical period.

Now, anyone who is familiar with these works will recognize that they can not casually be lumped together as representatives of Scandinavian traditio-historical research in the sense advocated by Engnell. Only the two first-named works, those of Ahlström and Carlson, were written under the personal influence of Engnell and according to the guidelines established by him[20]. In Grønbæk's work the specifically "Scandinavian" thrust is only present in two central emphases, and in Mettinger's book only the choice of themes is reminiscent of the programme of Scandinavian tradition history, whereas his procedure is not. For this reason, in what follows I shall direct my principal attention to the works of Ahlström and Carlson, and only secondarily be concerned with those of Grønbæk and Mettinger.

Ahlström's examination of the eighty-ninth psalm may be regarded as an attempt to test the thesis of Engnell according to which the Israelites were held to have adopted sacral kingship from the Canaanites during the reign of David, and to have elevated it to the status of a central "topos" of their own religion. Thus Ps 89 is regarded as probably originally having been an old Jebusite liturgy which belonged to the (hypothetical) ritual for the renewal of life, and which was adapted by the Israelites to their new circumstances (Ahlström, pp. 141f. 152f). The Sitz im Leben of the psalm in its Israelite version is held by Ahlström to be a ritual of the New Year Festival in which the king as *deus incarnatus* suffers, "dies", and "resurrects"[21]. Although Ahlström admits that the "resurrection" in question is nowhere mentioned in the psalm, he affirms that it belonged to the succeeding phase of the ritual (pp. 161f). Here Ahlström also agrees with his former teacher, Engnell, in detecting behind the name "David" a Canaanite fertility deity, *Dod*, whose name David, that is, the quondam Elhanan (2 Sam 21:19), had assumed in Jerusalem, and to whom the original ritual underlying Ps 89 had once applied (pp. 163-173). Ahlström arrives at this conclusion via an exegesis which is not undemanding of its readers: the form-critical approach inaugurated by Gunkel is rejected in toto (pp. 9f), and in its place Ahlström derives from the superscription *maśkîl* a formal determination, which, according to Ahlström, demonstrates the attachment of the psalm to the (hypothetical) ritual of life-renewal (pp. 21-26), just as the antiquity of the psalm is taken for granted and its problematical relationship to the prose parallel in 2 Sam 7 is solved by the assertion that 2 Sam 7 represents an "historicized coronation liturgy" of younger date (p. 184). The seemingly historical features of, for example, the lament in v. 39-46 are explained away by means of a mythological interpretation (pp. 139-153), and expressions in the perfect tense are translated in the present throughout (p. 131), which gives the psalm a timeless character. Finally, the speaker of the concluding lament in v. 39-46 and the prayer in v. 47-52 is identified with the king (p. 174), which is a necessary though by no means obvious presupposition for interpreting the work as a royal psalm.

If one is to evaluate the viability of the theses concerning sacral kingship in Israel which have been proposed by adherents of Engnell's school, the work of Ahlström on psalm exegesis must be accorded considerable significance, since according to Engnell's supporters the Psalms provide "the clearest expressions of the essential nature and fundamental motifs of Israelite religion" (Ahlström 1962, p. 206)[22]. This would be contested by such critics as M. Noth, who operates on the basis of the historical traditions.

Methodologically considered, Ahlström is in every way a faithful follower of the principles laid down by Engnell. This is evident already at the text-critical level, where he displays an extremely conservative attitude towards the MT. Thus he synoptically prints out the text of the psalm in Hebrew, Greek, Syriac, and Latin, but it is all a sham fight, as Mowinckel somewhat wickedly remarked (Mowinckel 1960,

p. 296), since Ahlström only undertakes to alter the MT at two points
(v. 20 and 51). Paradoxically enough, both of these corrections take
place in passages where a change in the Massoretic vocalization is not
required. In v. 20 Ahlström (p. 99) changes the pl. *la-ḥᵃsīdēkā*, "to
your pious ones" against the MT and all the Versions to a sg. *la-
ḥᵃsīdᵉkā*, "to your pious one", and thus refers the expression to the
king, who then becomes the recipient of the subsequent oracle (v.
20b- 38). Similarly, in v. 51 he transforms the pl. *ᵃbādēkā*, "your
servants", according to the witness of twenty-four Hebrew manuscripts and the Syriac translation to the sg. *ᵃbdᵉkā*, "your servant",
which he regards as a self-designation of the royal singer (pp. 154f).
Neither of these corrections is in any way necessary. Both *ḥᵃsīdēkā*
and *ᵃbādēkā* are frequently used epithets for the Israelite people in
the literature of the psalms[23], and occur, e.g. in Ps 79:2 in parallelis-
mus membrorum: "They have cast the dead bodies of your *servants* ...
the flesh of *your pious ones* to the wild beasts of the earth."

   Although these concepts do not figure in parallelism in Ps 89, they
do nevertheless illuminate each other reciprocally: Yahweh's promise
of eternal rule to the Davidides was once, according to v. 20, pronounced to the people of Yahweh, for which reason another writer has
conceived the idea of appealing as a member of the same people to
this ancient assurance in time of crisis. If this be admitted, there is
then no possibility of regarding the singer as a royal personality,
which makes considerable difficulties for Ahlström's interpretation
(cf. Veijola 1982, pp. 113-117)[24].

   Moreover, for Ahlström the unity of the psalm is an axiom which
requires no substantiation. But the decision as to the unity or dis-
unity of a text is a *literary critical* task, which, however, is never a
real possibility according to Engnell's method. It is striking that in Ps
89 in v. 4-5 God suddenly speaks in 1. p.sg. and in these two verses
adumbrates a theme which is thoroughly explored in the subsequent
oracle (v. 20b-38). In addition to this, it can not be without significance for the literary-critical analysis that the stichoi in the respective parts of the psalm are of quite different lengths[25]. Nor is it helpful to attempt to account for the different lengths of the stichoi in
the hymn in v. 2-3.6-19, and in the divine oracle in v. 20-38, respectively, by reference to the liturgical use of the psalm. Even if this be
maintained, it is still striking that in one passage no metrical distinction is made where the divine oracular speech shifts into a human la-

ment (v. 39ff.), while elsewhere the last part of the human speech (v. 47-52) quite clearly separates itself from the preceding materials.

I submit that the most probable explanation of all this unevenness consists in the solution that the psalm was composed in three successive phases. The first stage of this development was an ancient hymn (v. 2-3. 6-19), which was expanded by later editing by the addition of an oracle (v. 20-38) and a lament (v. 39-46). The same hand will also have composed v. 4-5 which declare the theme of the oracle and thus connect it with the hymn. In the third phase the poem thus developed was supplied with a forceful petition (v. 47-52) (cf. Veijola 1982, pp. 32-46).

Furthermore, the determination of the relationship of Ps 89 to other, both poetical and historical texts is a literary-critical task of some promise. Let us take as our example the relationship of Ps 89 to 2 Sam 7, since most commentators have stressed the priority of the historical text (cf. Veijola 1982, p. 60, n.1), while Ahlström emphasizes the psalm. It appears that on this question the Scandinavians are united against the majority opinion; already prior to Ahlström Mowinckel had embraced this view (Mowinckel 1947, p. 224), and he was subsequently joined by both Carlson (1964, p. 121) and Grønbæk (1971, p. 35, n.107). Mettinger (1976, pp. 255f) was indeed the first to break ranks and decide the question of dependence in the opposite direction, in my opinion correctly. A careful comparison of 2 Sam 7 and Ps 89 namely shows that Ps 89 presupposes 2 Sam 7 in its present form and in fact at numerous points the psalm reveals both a younger terminology and is theologically more developed (cf. Veijola 1982, pp. 60-69). We may consider the references in Ps 89 to election and covenantal theology as our examples (v. 4.20.29.35.40); these are entirely absent in 2 Sam 7 and, conversely, are characteristic of (late) exilic theology[26]. If one further considers that, for example, Carlson regards 2 Sam 7 as an entirely Deuteronomistic creation, a view, incidentally, which is most likely somewhat too sweeping (see below), it becomes difficult to avoid the conclusion that Ps 89 must be younger still. It is thus correct of Mettinger to date the psalm to the latter part of the Exile (Mettinger 1976, p. 279).

Now, if the psalm derives from a period without kings, can it be seriously argued that it has to do with the Monarchy and its sacred institutions? This leads us to the question of the determination of form. Ahlström nonchalantly ignores the formal analyses undertaken by

Gunkel and announces that the latter had in his approach to the psalms of lament pursued his system to absurd lengths (p. 9), and with this justification he takes as his own point of departure the superscriptions to the psalms. This leads him into a maelstrom of wild hypotheses in which the unknown is explained by the likewise unknown. For example, the *maśkīl* is designated a New Year Festival psalm belonging to the ritual of life-renewal. But this conclusion has nothing to do with the meaning of the word; rather, it is derived from the contents of a number of psalms which have been interpreted according to Ahlström's theory[27], and I regard this conclusion as inevitably circular.

Ahlström pays dutiful homage to Engnell by embracing the latter's "Dwd-David" theory, according to which the *leḏāwīd* psalms will originally have belonged to the cult of the Canaanite divinity, *Dod*. But apart from the sheer improbability of this supposition[28] the question simply begs to be asked as to why psalm 89 does *not* bear this superscription, if it really is the psalm par excellence of this group. Nor does Ps 89 possess the superscription *lamnasseah*, the (hypothetically) North Israelite parallel to *leḏāwīd* (cf. Engnell 1969, p. 86).

Although Gunkel did not undertake a thorough form and Gattungscritical interpretation of this psalm[29], his system nevertheless offers a sound basis for a satisfactory formal determination. Ps 89 is composed of the typical elements of a collective psalm of lamentation; it begins with a *hymnic* section (v. 2-3.6-19), which is not unusual in a collective lament[30]. A divine oracle follows (v. 20-38), whose function is to reflect on *God's earlier saving actions*, and the *lament* itself (v. 39-46), formulated as an accusation against God, stands in contrast to this. Again, consonant with the demands of style, the collective lament is rounded off with a petition (v. 47-52) (cf. Veijola 1982, pp. 120-133).

The content of Ps 89 does not argue against this form-critical analysis. The grand promises concerning the future of the Davidides now belong to the past, as the introduction to the oracle (v. 20a) unequivocally shows ("*Then* you *spoke*....")[31]. The *lament* (v. 39-46) indicated what is left of the original promise: it has been annulled, the royal crown has been dashed to the ground (v. 40), the fortresses have been laid in ruins (v. 41), Judah's neighbours have plundered and mocked her at will (v. 42). The opponents have been ultimately successful, while Israel's own king has been deprived of throne and sceptre (v. 45) and heaped with scorn (v. 46). It is quite impossible that this picture should describe a reference to any ritual humiliation of the king; rather, here we have to do with references to the *historical* experiences (e.g. Mowinckel 1960, p. 295) to which Judah was subjected in connexion with and subsequent to 587. Moreover, this conclusion is also supported by the vocabulary of the psalm, which recurs in other exilic literature describing this same catastrophe (demonstrated in extenso in Veijola 1982, pp. 95-112).

Finally, it is worth emphasizing that the psalm clearly has a collective character; where the literal level makes reference to the king, in reality the whole interest of the psalm concentrates around the *people*. Closer examination shows that this is not only true of the lament, but of the entire final (exilic) form of the psalm. The epithets "your anointed one" (v. 39.52) and "my/your servant" (v. 4.21.40) also serve this collective tendency. In the nineteenth century the collective interpretation of this psalm was very widely accepted[32]; it has recently been reaffirmed by the studies of J. Becker (especially 1977, pp. 573f), and deserves greater recognition than it has as yet received[33].

By way of summary, as my cursory remarks have indicated, it appears that the thesis that David imported the apparatus of divine kingship into Israel can not gain support from this psalm; nor can it be shown to refer to an (hypothetical) ritual humiliation of the king in the course of the New Year Festival. Otherwise, we would have to postulate such a thorough "democratization" of the original psalm that we would have no possibility whatsoever to discover the former nucleus of the psalm behind its present form.

Carlson's programme is more modest than that of Ahlström in that he does not attempt to demonstrate the correctness of particular Engnellian theses. Instead, he merely attempts to analyze the materials of the Second Book of Samuel along methodological lines laid down by Engnell. The latter had regarded the study of the variety of Old Testament compositional techniques as an important aspect of traditio-historical analysis (see above), and this project was undertaken in full by Carlson. He painstakingly recorded such compositional practices as repetition, ring-composition, key words, and association, as well as those of anticipatory and retrospective passages. Thus he arrived at the by no means obvious conclusion that the Second Book of Samuel was altogether a product of Deuteronomistic composition. Carlson's "D-group" attributed to David a typological function, and they depicted him under two complementary aspects: in 2 Sam 2-7 under the Blessing, for which reason the Deuteronomistic chapter 2 Sam 7 is accorded great significance; and in 2 Sam 9-24 he appears under the Curse, which he incurs as a consequence of his role in the Bathsheba affair (pp. 24f). Carlson finds that the number seven is accorded an important part in the composition, and he repeatedly assumes points of contact with the Ugaritic epic of King Keret (p. 34)[34]. The author rejects the possibility of such ancient complexes as a History of David's Rise or a Succession Narrative, and instead presupposes a pre-Deuteronomistic epic of David (pp. 43.47f.189f.263). However, he makes no attempt to define this hypothetical work more closely.

Carlson's work is remarkable in at least one respect: he was the first to hypothecate, in contradistinction to M. Noth, a comprehensive Deuteronomistic revision of the Books of Samuel. As is well known, Noth's view — which has won general acceptance — was that the Deuteronomists were responsible for the negative evaluations of the Monarchy in 1 Sam 8-12, while they had otherwise only marginally reworked the Saul and David traditions (Noth 1943, pp. 61-66). Against this, Carlson attributed the entire composition in its present form to the "D-group", and reckoned with numerous sections which had been edited by the Deuteronomists themselves[35]. It is also noteworthy that 2 Sam 21-24 and Jdg 17-21, which Noth had regarded as post-Deuteronomistic "appendices", are taken by Carlson to be components of the Deuteronomistic composition (pp. 141.227). These insights are noteworthy, more especially so as scholars both before and after Carlson have failed to register them. It is accordingly necessary to enquire as to why Carlson's conclusions have won so little attention as they have; the reason, to put it briefly, has to do with the author's way of arriving at them.

I have no theoretical objections to Carlson's approach to textual criticism; one does, however, note considerable liberalization vis à vis the positions of Engnell and Ahlström. The author recognizes the poor condition of the MT and the correspondingly high value of the LXX witness for the study of the Books of Samuel (Carlson 1964, pp. 36f). Accordingly, Carlson undertakes numerous corrections of the MT in the course of his work, one of which, in a crucial passage, is indeed rather audacious. In the Parable of Nathan in 2 Sam 12:6 David pronounces a judgement upon himself, which, according to the MT, requires *fourfold* restitution for theft. This judgement agrees with the corresponding regulation in the Book of the Covenant (Exod 21: 37; cf. further Lk 19: 8); nevertheless, Carlson rejects the Massoretic reading in favour of the "sevenfold" of LXX[BA](pp. 154-157). His reasons for doing so are more "ideological" than text-critical: Carlson needs a sevenfold punishment because of the seven-scheme which, in his opinion, plays a central role in the Deuteronomistic composition. Here textual criticism is subordinated all too strongly to the criterion of content. Moreover, it should not be allowed to pass without comment that Carlson's seven-scheme would remain unsatisfactory even if his LXX reading of 2 Sam 12: 6 was correct, since he holds that this scheme is also realized in the account of David's life, and to this end adds together two incidental date notices in 2 Sam 15: 7 and 2 Sam 21:1 in order to arrive at a numerologically satisfactory figure (pp. 167f) – and yet, these notices are completely unrelated. Finally, it is not a little strange to be told that 2 Sam 24 also belongs to David's "sevenfold" punishment (p. 204), although this chapter lies outside the compass of Carlson's postulated seven-year cycle!

But it is Carlson's attitude towards literary criticism and to the closely related problem of oral tradition that ultimately raises fundamental problems. The author does not onesidedly assert the authority of the oral tradition; rather, like Engnell in his later writings he treats the oral and written traditions as complementary quantities (Carlson 1964, p. 16). However, Carlson does emphasize the primacy of oral tradition with respect to its reliability, and feels that both the compositional and redactional work were based upon oral traditions (pp. 17f). This entails a strict rejection of literary criticism (pp. 9-11), and the traditio-historical method is characterized as "an analytical alternative to literary criticism" (p. 10) which is capable of achieving the synthesis neglected by literary criticism (p. 35). In short, Carlson undertakes redaction criticism without prior literary-critical analysis, and this, I submit, is a methodologically indefensible procedure.

This fact emerges already in Carlson's selection of units to be more closely examined, for the author by no means intends to treat all the materials in the Second Book of Samuel; rather, in actual fact he only discusses the exegesis of certain isolated sections without informing the reader as to his criteria for selecting them (cf. Richter 1966, p. 138). Why, for example, is the entire Absalom story only cursorily dealt with, and the first two chapters of the First Book of Kings, which by Carlson's own admission are closely bound up with the preceding materials (pp. 189f), completely left out of account? A preliminary literary analysis would here have formed the basis for an intelligible synthetic understanding of the formation of the final product.

Even more important is the fact that, like Engnell before him, Carlson operates with a Deuteronomistic Historical Work stretching from Deut to the end of the Second Book of Kings (Carlson 1964, p. 22)[36], and in reality this construct resides on a literary-critical foundation. This is fully evident in the work of M. Noth, whose *Überlieferungsgeschichtliche Studien* I (1943) Engnell made liberal use of (Engnell 1945, pp. 231-46), while paradoxically dismissing Noth's literary criticism (p. 210, n.3), even though it formed the backbone of Noth's work. One must furthermore consider that in this connexion Noth himself stood on the shoulders of none other than the much-execrated J. Wellhausen, who had already in large measure separated the Deuteronomic parts in the historical books from the older traditions (Wellhausen 1899, pp. 116-134.208-301). If one denies the literary-critical foundation, the entire edifice collapses. To take but one example: it is a major dictum of Engnell and his students that the negative evaluation of the Monarchy in 1 Sam *8-12 derives from the Deuteronomists (Engnell 1945, p. 239)[37]. But how do we know this? We know it first once we have observed certain repetitions and contradictions in these narratives and have explained them by the presumption of a number of literary stages which, again, must be related to a total picture — whether evolutionistic or not — of the history and literature of ancient Israel (cf. Wellhausen 1899, pp. 240-243; Noth 1943, pp. 54-60). Should one question this procedure in principle, the negative attitude of the Deuteronomists to the Monarchy becomes a purely "ideological" postulate without basis for verification in the sources.

The lack of a literary-critical analysis in Carlson's work leaves the reader without any indication as to *why* certain passages are designated "Deuteronomistic". The author's criteria appear to be "ideology" and terminology. In 2 Sam 7 and 2 Sam 12:1-12, for example, it is principally "ideological" factors which lead Carlson to assign them to the Deuteronomists (pp. 60.104f.157f). On other occasions such terms as *nāgīd* (pp. 52-53), *bāhar* (p. 65), and *menūhā* (pp. 100-103) are decisive, while at still other times Carlson seems tacitly to accept the arguments of the literary critics[38].

By means of these procedures, Carlson arrives at isolated striking conclusions, as noted above, but for the most part he hangs fire, as, for example, when he outright declines to acknowledge the literarily secondary character of the Deuteronomistic sections. One could take as an example Carlson's treatment of 2 Sam 5:1-2, for here he desires on the one hand to postulate Deuteronomistic influence because of the title *nāgīd*, while on the other he contests the apparent doublet at the beginning of verses 1 and 3 (the two visits of the tribes and elders of Israel, respectively, to David in Hebron) as a literary-critical criterion (p. 55). Thus his result based on this methodologically curious procedure is a strange sort of *sic et non*: the passage is simultaneously Deuteronomistic and non-Deuteronomistic! And yet, in a word, there are both external and internal indications which imply the Deuteronomistic provenance of the entire passage in 2 Sam 5:1-2 (cf. Veijola 1975, pp. 63-66).

In some cases Carlson's failure to employ literary criticism has resulted in his attributing more to his "D-group" than is probable or demonstrable. The most obvious example of this is 2 Sam 7, which is regarded by him as altogether a Deuteronomistic product, although its background is seen as rooted in the ideology of divine kingship (Carlson 1964, p. 60). This is a generalization which does not take into account the very complex character of this chapter. Among others, T.N. D. Mettinger, with whose reading of this chapter I am not in complete agreement, has detected indications that the chapter has undergone a succession of reworkings on the way to its final form (Mettinger 1976, pp. 48-63)[39]. Again, in the case of 2 Sam 7 it is easy to show that the "D-group" could not possibly have been so homogeneous an aggregation as is supposed by Engnell and Carlson[40], rather, it was composed of separate tendencies, each with its characteristic emphasis, and which are susceptible to differentiation by literary-critical means. In 2 Sam 7 the first Deuteronomistic layer, DtrH, has transformed the ancient assurance to the accedant to the throne (v. 8a[*].9a.12.14.15. 17)[41] into a dynastic promise of "eternal" character (v. 11b.13.16. 18-21.27aβ.b-29), while his late exilic successor, DtrN, has reapplied it to the people of Israel (v. 1b.6.7.8b.9b-11a.22-27aα)(Veijola 1982, pp. 62-65.144f).

An odd by-product of Carlson's neglect of literary criticism is the subordinate role played by actual tradition history in his study. Thus he occasionally speaks of the prehistory of the traditions, notably in

connexion with the account of the Ark in 2 Sam 6, where he detects
earlier connexions with fertility rituals (pp. 66-68.70.94f), and also
in conjunction with the Bathsheba narrative in 2 Sam 10-12, which is
allegedly a historicized Sukkoth tradition referring to booths, *hieros
gamos*, and sham fight (p. 144). It is nevertheless clear that here we
have only to do with sporadic remarks and assertions which can not
qualify as serious attempts to prove such extraordinary theses. Nor
should this astonish us, when we recall that Carlson affirms the thesis
of the high reliability of oral tradition (p. 16), and he then considers
the study of the composition as his actual task. Is it not a sort of *con-
tradictio in adiecto* when the author suddenly reckons with completely different sorts of stages in the prehistory of his texts?

On the other hand, it is consistent of him to reject the possibility
of reconstructing his hypothetical ancient epic of David, since apparently according to Carlson it will have existed in oral form, and the
possibility of pinpointing it more exactly is extremely remote. But as
for the scholar who allows for the possibility that written tradition
may have been active already at the pre-Deuteronomistic level, he has
a promising programme ahead of him, consisting of the attempt to illuminate the character of these pre-Deuteronomistic Davidic traditions, and thus in a real sense also to discover their tradition history.

J.H. Grønbœk has made a praiseworthy effort in this direction in
his study of the history of David's rise to power. He arrives at the conclusion that there was such a history of David's rise, and that it extended from 1 Sam 15:1 to 2 Sam 5:10. Grønbæk assigns this work to
a purposeful author whose raw materials were various, but principally
of an oral nature (Grønbæk 1971, p. 17). His goal will then have been,
"so to represent the course of events that David did not accede to the
throne as an usurper, but to the contrary as the legitimate and sole
conceivable successor to King Saul" (p. 19). Grønbæk dates the composition of the history of David's rise to shortly after the partition of
the Solomonic kingdom (p. 277), and holds that Rehoboam was able
to profit "ideologically" from the work in his conflict with the northern tribes (p. 276).

It will neither be possible nor necessary in these pages to discuss
the thesis of Grønbæk in detail. His theses are by no means so distinctively "Scandinavian" as are those of Ahlström and Carlson. Moreover, Grønbæk's results agree in numerous points with the views A.

Weiser (1966) had already published on the history of David's rise. Grønbæk's version of tradition history displays its "Scandinavian" colouring in two respects: first, he takes exception to the methods of literary criticism, which he regards as dated because of the failure of source-critical explanations to deal with the Books of Samuel (Grønbæk 1971, pp. 30.259f). Against source criticism Grønbæk proposes his own method, which he designates as "tradition-critical" and "traditio-historical analysis" (p. 17). In practice this means that Grønbæk attributes the palpable unevenness of the narratives to the traditions which the author took over as well as he could. Later redactions such as, for example, that of the Deuteronomists, are allowed only a modest role (p. 271)[42]. Thus a picture of a history of David's rise emerges which had attained its present form as early as the tenth century, and which was only slightly revised subsequently.

This picture, which Mettinger has largely adopted (1976, pp. 36-47), seems to me to be an over-simplification of the heterogeneous literary and traditio-historical character of the history of David's rise. For example, I should regard as most unlikely the proposition that the account of Saul's rejection in 1 Sam 15 and of David's anointment by Samuel in 1 Sam 16:1-13 already existed in the tenth century, and that they composed the beginning of the history of David's rise. I am sceptical because (a) the character of these texts shows them to belong to a much later, reflective phase of Israelite historiography, and (b) because they are unintelligible without the preceding Saulide traditions (Veijola 1975, p. 102, n.156)[43]. Moreover, the history of David's rise refers to passages outside of itself at several points[44], which indicates that it was probably further reworked after it had been combined with other Saulide and Davidic traditions – and this can first have occurred, according to Grønbæk (p. 16), in the course of Deuteronomistic redaction.

Grønbæk's second "Scandinavian" characteristic is his persistent interest in royal ideology, which he sees as having played godfather to a variety of different historical traditions (pp. 63f)[45]. Thus he senses the royal cult of the Jerusalem Temple behind the account of David's anointing in 1 Sam 16:1-13 (p. 75), just as he finds a historified myth which he supposes to reflect the battle of the king with the forces of chaos, whose Sitz im Leben will have been the cult of the New Year Festival, behind the narrative of David's insane behaviour at the court of Achish, king of Gath, in 1 Sam 21:11-16 (p. 145). Here and elsewhere the presence of features of the royal ideology is regarded as likely on the basis of echoes in the Psalms[46]. It is impossible to prove the contrary here, since Grønbæk also neglects to substantiate his arguments more fully. However, the experiences we garnered in connexion with our examination of the relationship of Ps 89 to 2 Sam 7 indicate that one may not unreflectively assign psalms which bear traces of royal ideology to the early monarchical period, and then regard them as examplars for the historical traditions. In the example cited, at any rate, we noted that the psalm to the contrary betrays its dependence on the historical tradition. It is quite another question as to just how "sacral" the early Israelite monarchy in reality was.

Mettinger has recently dealt intensively with this latter problem in his sizeable monograph, and he has arrived at some conclusions which are germane to this discussion. It is not by chance that Mettinger first deals with the civil legitimation of the king, since he sees this as enjoying historical priority to the sacral form. Thus Mettinger holds that many later actions and concepts originally were profane in nature, and that theological use was first made of them in later times (Mettinger 1976, pp. 295f). For example, the author regards the royal anointment as originally a contractual act, in which the people placed themselves under obligation to their king (2 Sam 2:4; 5:3). It will first have been during the reign of Solomon, whose right to the throne was not confirmed by a popular assembly, that anointment evolved into a sacral rite (1 Kgs 1:39), which was subsequently retrojected on to the figures of Saul (1 Sam 9:1-10:16) and David (1 Sam 16:1-13)(pp. 230-232). Mettinger finds a later product of this development in the "Davidic covenant", which he claims did not receive explicit formulation before the Exile (2 Sam 23:5; Ps 89:4.29.35.40; Jer 33:21; 2 Chr 13:4; 21:7)(pp. 275-290; 292).

A similar development is held to apply to the *nāgīd* designation, which in Mettinger's view will originally have been a secular term which was first employed in 1 Kgs 1:35 to describe Solomon as David's designated successor (= *nāgīd*)[47]. The title will have been adopted subsequently, in the last decades of the tenth century, by northern prophetic circles, who gave the term theological significance (1 Sam 9:16; 10:1). From the north the title returned in its new trappings to Judah, where the author of the History of David's Rise incorporated it as a sacral title applying to David (1 Sam 25:30; 2 Sam 5:2; 6:21; 7:8) (pp. 182f).

In this connexion Mettinger's insight into the "high-messianic" passages, which express faith in the abiding rule of the Davidic dynasty (e.g. 1 Sam 25:28-31; 2 Sam 5:1-2; 6:21; 7:8-9.11b.14b-15.16[*]. 18-22a.27-29), is interesting, in that he notes their redactional character (p.295). Thus, although the author does not contest the antiquity of the conception of the king as God's (adoptive) son (2 Sam 7:14; Ps 2:7)(p. 291), his work clearly suggests that the sacral character of the Israelite monarchy was not cut from whole cloth in the dawn of time, but that it must have been the result of evolutionary growth.

However, there is some question as to whether Mettinger allows sufficient time for this development to take place, since, according to him, the greater part of the literary activity described above will have occurred in the Solomonic period, or shortly thereafter. Thus the objections offered above to Grønbæk's scheme are also fundamentally applicable to Mettinger's early dating. Nevertheless, Mettinger's openness to literary-critical considerations leads him to admit somewhat more elbowroom to the Deuteronomistic redaction than Grønbæk does[48]. Thus a peculiar traditio-historical diastasis is observable in his work: themes which were intensively treated towards the end of the tenth century will have been revived three and a half centuries later when the discussion was continued exactly at the point where it had stopped centuries before. If this excessive chronological span is to be foreshortened in any way, it will be at the upper end of the scale.

To all this I would object that the Solomonic age did not offer such favourable preconditions for the development of "high-messianic" and other sacrally legitimating theologoumena. This is already conspicuous in the original Davidic Succession Narrative, which Mettinger correctly dates to the age of Solomon (p. 31), even though he somewhat anachronistically follows L. Rost in viewing this work as a composition written *ad majorem gloriam Salomonis* (Mettinger 1976, p. 31). However, recent studies have clearly shown that the work is introduced by an unequivocally anti-Davidic section (2 Sam [*]10-12) (Würthwein 1974, pp. 19-32; Veijola 1979) and concludes on a no less anti-Solomonic note (1 Kgs [*]1-2)[49]. Accordingly, it is hardly likely that the Davidic dynasty will simultaneously have been glorified by the attribution of exuberantly sacral characteristics. To the contrary, even the profane character of the old Succession Narrative strengthens the conclusion achieved by Mettinger that its "sacral kingship" aspect was a product of later, rather than Solomonic, tradition. Of course, this conclusion is diametrically opposed to the theses of Engnell and Ahlström adumbrated above.

Stock-taking and Future Perspectives

In conclusion, then, we should enquire as to what remains of the studies of the Davidic traditions which have been carried out according to Engnell's traditio-historical method. The point of departure for Engnell's methodological considerations was the presupposition that traditions were transmitted for a long time orally prior to being written down very late. This hypothesis was shared by Ahlström and Carlson, but not by Grønbæk and Mettinger, who saw the recording of the Davidic traditions as having taken place not long after their origination. In this connexion I would be prone to go some of the way with Engnell and Carlson and allow some leeway to the living oral and written process of tradition.

After Engnell, the conservative textual criticism resulting from the assumption of the great reliability of the oral tradition was recognized in principle by Ahlström alone, who, however, did not observe the principle in practice. Since Carlson's work Scandinavian scholars no longer regard the MT, at least as far as the Books of Samuel are concerned, as sacrosanct; instead, they correct the text where necessary with the aid of the Versions, above all honouring the LXX and Qumran texts. In this respect the attitude of Scandinavian scholars no longer differs from that of their brethren in other lands.

The most enduring characteristic of the Scandinavians has been their negative evaluation of literary criticism. From Engnell to Grønbæk, the literary-critical method has been strictly rejected, and traditio-historical method has remained the preferred alternative. This has been a fateful error, and it has led to an artificial opposition between the two methods. One must agree with H. Gressmann that "Textual and literary criticism (are) still the presuppositions without which one can only construct fabulous castles in the air, hypotheses without scientific significance" (1924, p. 3). But whoever accepts this statement does not need to deny the justification for other methods such as tradition history. Gressmann himself, who wrote the passage cited above, also very energetically protested elsewhere against a monolithic literary criticism. "Under the advocacy of Wellhausen, literary criticism has experienced an extraordinary series of successes. We, too, are aware that we are standing on the shoulders of previous generations, and we thankfully acknowledge their achievements. However, it is impossible any longer to close our eyes to the fact that literary criticism alone —and thus the school of Wellhausen —has exhausted its role"[50]. For Gressmann, as for Gunkel, this conclusion did not lead to the rejection of literary criticism, but to its completion with the aid of the new method of tradition history. Indeed, how could one in any way study the received written and oral traditions without previously clarifying their literary position in their respective contexts, and their external form? If these initial literary, formal, and Gattungs-critical considerations are ignored[51], the pursuit of tradition history becomes like a blind leap into a murky abyss, or else it arrives at no results whatsoever.

Scandinavian historians of tradition have had fewer fundamental reservations about redaction criticism than they have about literary criticism, since indeed a step in this direction was already present in Engnell's requirement for synthesis. However, Carlson's work illustrates with abundant clarity that fact that redactio-historical synthesis becomes irremediably impenetrable if it is not preceded by literary-critical analysis.

My remarks here will hopefully demonstrate that "tradition history" in Engnell's sense provides no pass-key, no sovereign alternative, to literary criticism or to other exegetical methods; it is a method among others. Therefore, to cite the words of H. Ringgren, "What we require today is a synthesis in which all practices and methods conjoin to enable us to reach our common goal, namely the reconstruction of the milieux which produced the texts, and the functions which they will have fulfilled, in order to grasp their real meaning" (1966, col. 647).

THE TRADITIO-HISTORICAL
STUDY OF THE PROPHETS

A.S. Kapelrud

In his book *The Traditions of Israel,* D.A. Knight (1973) says: "Of all the Old Testament scholars affected by the traditio-historical direction taken by many of the Uppsala scholars, Kapelrud and Nielsen are probably the ones who have been the strongest influenced by this approach." (p.351).

I shall allow this quotation to serve as background for the fact that I have taken upon me the comprehensive task of accounting for traditio-historical research into the prophets. It will only be possible in these pages to give some fleeting impressions of the considerable material available in this area.

In my own case, it is not difficult to see where the foundations were laid. Even if Mowinckel was strongly influenced by the litera-ry-critical method, he seldom refrained from emphasizing the oral tradition which underlay the existing texts. But the decisive impulse came with H.S. Nyberg's *Studien zum Hoseabuche* (1935). The way Nyberg attacked various problems made a deep impression which appeared to me, who was at the time a twenty-three year-old student, as a virtual revelation, so that I strongly desired to make better acquaintance with this path of study. Even if Nyberg had largely confined himself to texts in the Book of Hosea, he emphasized that the fundament was the oral tradition which had been dominant until as late as the time of the Exile (1935, p.8). The writing-down of the materials was primarily an aid to the oral tradition, which remained the basis (p.128), and which persisted even after written fixation. It was possible to investigate the process of tradition, but it was quite impossible, according to Nyberg, to arrive at the *ipsissima verba* of the prophet. In reality, Nyberg formulated a number of theses which it became the task of his heirs to check and to substantiate more thoroughly. This was in fact done, even if Nyberg's theses met a certain degree of resistance, especially on the Continent.

The first to pursue Nyberg's pioneering work was Harris Birkeland, whose little booklet, *Zum hebräischen Traditionswesen,* appeared in 1938. In his introduction Birkeland, like Nyberg before him, referred to Arabic traditions and oral transmission. Birkeland emphasized that the glossary of terms used in the study of the composition of the prophetic books included such expressions as "tradition", "complexes", and "circles", instead of, as previously, "notices", "large literary products", and "scribes at their desks" (1938, p. 22). If one enquired at all as to the *ipsissima verba* of the prophets, this was only conceivable in traditio-historical rather than literary-critical terms.

The confusing disorder in the prophetic books is thus simply explained, according to Birkeland: it represents the written fixation of an oral tradition. Occasionally, individual complexes will have been combined with each other, or different versions of them may have been preserved. The prophetic books were seen to contain materials stemming from a variety of originally small circles which developed into larger groups where the texts grew and finally became the property of Judaism through a process of continual selection.

In the last part of his book, Birkeland offered a concise sketch of the composition of the prophetic books; he did not attempt to explain how the various complexes had originated. However, one can not avoid noticing that Birkeland's results correspond very closely to those arrived at by literary-critical methods. This is perhaps not so strange after all, but at any rate it is clear that Birkeland himself was so strongly influenced by the older method that he was not able to escape from its confinement as fully as he may have wished.

The next scholar to follow in Nyberg's footsteps was the dynamic and temperamental Ivan Engnell. In his introductory work, *Gamla Testamentet I* (1945), Engnell affirmed the importance of the oral tradition, and he asserted that the Old Testament had largely existed in its collected form at the oral stage, prior to its being written down.

Engnell concerned himself specifically with the composition of the prophetic books in an article in *Svensk exegetisk årsbok* (1947), entitled "Profetia och tradition". The article appeared in response to Mowinckel's little book, *Prophecy and Tradition* (Mowinckel 1946), which was a continuation of an article he had published in *Norsk teologisk tidsskrift* (1942), "Oppkomsten av profetlitteraturen". Mowinckel noted here that the words of the prophets were preserved by means of oral tradition, and that the prophetic books were based on oral materials. However, Mowinckel felt that the oral tradition could not be regarded as reliable, and that the disciples of the prophets, especially those of Isaiah, had contributed to reformulate his prophecies of judgement into nationalistic prophecies of salvation. While Birkeland agreed with this view-point, Engnell strongly opposed it and asserted that one could not presuppose such a contradictory relationship between a prophet and his disciples. Rather, as Engnell saw it, their prophecy had to be understood as a unity.

In reply to this Mowinckel claimed that research had to be accorded its entire freedom, among other things to attempt to rediscover the prophet's own words, to find out who the prophets actually were, and what they really said to people on the streets and in the market-places. These views again reveal that Mowinckel attached scant faith to the oral tradition, and also that he especially saw the prophecies of salvation as later additions. Against these ideas, Engnell stressed that oral tradition was not an invariable quantity, that while popular tradition could - and does - often go amiss, the transmission of words deriving from a divine revelation was subjected to quite different, and more stringent, controls.

There was, however, one striking aspect which confused those of us who had eagerly sought Engnell's article; this was the modification of his theory the author in fact undertook when emphasizing the dominance of oral transmission in the prophetic books, for here Engnell revealed that he presupposed two types of prophetic literature. One of these he called the "liturgy type", the other the "diwān type", using an Arabic term as behooved a quondam disciple of Nyberg. Engnell assigned to the "liturgy type" such works as Joel, Nahum, Habakkuk, and Deutero-Isaiah. Here, according to Engnell, the materials had been created by the various prophets, who may well have written them down from the beginning. Thus such works were not formed in the course of a long process of oral transmission, even if they may have been transmitted orally in part.

The "diwān type", however, was held to be different; here we have to do with such figures as Amos, Hosea, Jeremiah, and proto-Isaiah. In these materia s we encounter the results of significant oral traditions, of prophetic words and accounts of the prophets' doings which were transmitted and distributed among disciples and tradents who collected materials pertaining to the prophets. In Engnell's opinion, this did not signify that we should be able to distinguish the words of the prophet in question from those of his disciples. The prophets were themselves able to proclaim both judgement and salvation, just as they were also capable of employing catchword association techniques, so that in reality we have no certain criteria for distinguishing between a prophet's own words and the later additions of his tradents.

On this point Mowinckel again objected, and asserted that the task was nevertheless to attempt to study the *history* of a given tradition, although in order to achieve this the scholar would be forced to adopt criteria whose validity was not recognized by Engnell. In short, Mowinckel felt that even if the process of tradition had been oral, it should be possible to trace the path of development.

Engnell was not able to present clear criteria for distinguishing between the "liturgy type" and the "diwān type" of transmission in either *Gamla Testamentet* or in "Profetia och tradition". He was, however, continually preoccupied with this problem, as we can see from the second edition of *Svenskt Bibliskt Uppslagsverk*, which was to be his last word on this and many other issues (1962-63 II, col.592; cf. 1969, p.166). Here Engnell admits that both designations have their unfortunate aspects. He says futher that the term "liturgy" is a purely formal literary designation which has no necessary relation to the cult, and adds that the prophetic "liturgy type" has a more thoroughly established poetic form; it is more creative, so that one senses the presence of the master behind the work.

This attempt at a definition leads Engnell into certain pitfalls, since he had himself already assigned several prophetic books with distinctively poetical characteristics to the "diwān type". He was forced to admit that a number of sections of the works in question, such as Amos 2-3, Hosea 5; 6; 9, Isaiah 3; 4; 5, and 10 were of the "liturgy type", but he emphasized that they belonged to larger contexts of the "diwān type". Furthermore, according to Engnell, the materials of the "diwān type" were less unified and their composition was somewhat loose. Both prophetic words and narratives about the prophets were assembled in this group, which is to say that many sorts of traditions were collected here. There was both poetry and prose, but there was no clear organization except for the alternating scheme of woe and weal, which was sometimes very systematically carried out. He assumed that behind a prophetic "diwān" lay a circle originally composed of prophetic disciples who were later replaced by other tradents. However, in Engnell's opinion it was the prophet who, as master, ultimately left his mark on the entirety of the collection; for this reason he still maintained that it was very difficult if not impossible to discern what belonged to the master and what to his disciples.

Naturally, it was in no way Engnell's intention that we should abandon our efforts at analysis; to the contrary, he insisted on the most thorough possible study of the texts, but without the prejudicial opinions which he felt so often characterized the literary-critical method. This last point was especially dear to Engnell, as he felt that the literary critics prevented themselves from arriving at a complete understanding of the texts. Many of the literary-critical insights were useful, but one would have to discount the evolutionistic viewpoints which had previously characterized the method.

Otherwise, Engnell insisted - like Mowinckel - that one should make use of all the available tools, be they form-critical, stylistic, philological, religio-historical, or motive-analytical, but he asserted that these methods should not be used to distinguish primary from secondary material. The analyst must always consider the synthesis represented by the existing form of the text. In Engnell's view, the totality was determined by the master.

Engnell was more precise as to his understanding of analysis in *SBU*; according to him, the internal interpretation had to take its point of departure in oral tradition. He counted such fundamental associative principles as those of doublets and variants; then there were the alternating scheme (weal and woe), iterative and retarding elements, parallelisms, and composition by inter-weaving of verses. The *Sitz im Leben* of the traditional materials, as well as their motives and tendencies, had also to be considered. Engnell emphasized that the process of the tradition was extremely conservative; the materials tended to be transmitted without allowing themselves to be influenced by extraneous cultural factors. Here Engnell was clearly reacting against the tendency to sociological argumentation which was already nascent many decades ago. In this connexion he was able to point to the conservative tendencies which had characterized the course of transmission within Judaism.

As far as comparative materials were concerned, Engnell warned against the use of Arabic sources, which he termed - with a thrust at Widengren - as "dangerous"; he felt rather that the Sumero-Akkadian literature provided the best comparative framework.

It has been necessary in the preceding pages to examine Engnell's understanding of traditio-historical research in detail, since his approach represented a clear break with earlier literary-critical attitudes and thus paved the way for new points of view. The fact that this research was unclear and ill-defined both as to its goals and its methods, as I have noted above, should not be allowed to obscure its merits. The pioneer who blazes new trails does not always know where they may lead; the task of clarification devolves upon posterity. I should perhaps also add that, in consideration of the ways the designation "tradition history" has been used by other scholars, its meaning is unfortunately not unequivocal. It has therefore been necessary to describe the Scandinavian form of the discipline, which has also attracted attention outside of Scandinavia.

In particular, it was the Scandinavian emphasis on oral tradition that won attention in the beginning; this is hardly surprising, when we consider how emphatically Nyberg, Mowinckel, and Birkeland had underlined its importance.

In 1952 H.H. Rowley of Manchester University, who was an alert observer of developments in Scandinavian Old Testament research, asked me if I could recommend for translation any one work or series of articles which might help to clarify the idea of tradition history which he mainly knew through Engnell. I suggested three articles in *Dansk teologisk Tidsskrift* on oral tradition written by the then-assistent-lecturer at Aarhus University, Eduard Nielsen (1950-52).

Nielsen's book, *Oral Tradition*, was published in London in 1954 with a preface by H.H. Rowley. Nielsen here explained the views underlying the Scandinavian emphasis on oral tradition. Moreover, he gave some examples of the use of traditio-historical method by subjecting to analysis Jer 36, a central chapter in the discussion on method, plus Micah 4-5 and Gen 6-9. Nielsen's textual analysis was very useful, as it contributed to an explanation of how traditio-historical research functioned in practice in the examination of texts which were controversial, at least to some degree.

Several Scandinavian works which were influenced by traditio-historical research appeared in the concluding years of the forties and on into the fifties. Such names as those of Haldar (1947), Kapelrud, Nielsen, Ringgren, and others belong to this period. Ringgren dealt with the question of oral tradition in an article in *Studia Theologica* (1949), entitled "Oral and Written Transmission in the O.T. Some Observations", and I employed traditio-historical method in my doctoral dissertation, *Joel Studies* (1948). *Shechem*, Eduard Nielsen's doctoral dissertation of 1955, was subtitled "A Traditio-Historical Investigation", and his work on the ten commandments in 1965 was correspondingly sub-titled "A Traditio-Historical Approach".

Nielsen offers some observations in the last-named work which point in the direction of the expanded concept of the discipline already advocated previously by Engnell in *SBU*. Nielsen declares that

> By the term 'traditio-historical' the author declares his adherence to a particular method of research. In its original form the material of the tradition under investigation was organically connected with a particular time and a particular place. As it now exists it has been separated from these and has become an element in a literary complex. Between these two stages in its development lie the numerous phases and epochs through which it has passed. It is taken that the special task of the traditio-historical approach is to trace the course of the material transmitted through these, examining each stage independently with the aim of determining its special interest, instead of (as happens all too often) concentrating exclusively upon the beginning and the end of the development. (E. Nielsen 1965, p.8, Eng. p. x).

Here I would underline a change of emphasis in relation to Engnell's position, for Nielsen strongly emphasizes the importance of the oral tradition while at the same time expanding the scope of what he terms traditio-historical research.

It would be impossible to say in this connexion how important were the criticisms which were launched against the emphasis on oral tradition. Resistance announced itself as early as 1947 with an article by the ultra-conservative J. van der Ploeg in *Revue biblique*, in which the author attacked the views of Mowinckel and Engnell. Yet another frontal assault appeared in the form of Geo Widengren's book, *Literary and Psychological Aspects of the Hebrew Prophets* (1948). Widengren made use of Arabic evidence to demonstrate that the written

AUGUSTANA UNIVERSITY COLLEGE
LIBRARY

tradition should be regarded as primary also in the case of Israel's prophets. Widengren later followed this initiative up with a corresponding
article in *Acta Orientalia* (1959). As mentioned above, Engnell rejected Widengren's Arabic evidence as irrelevant (1962-63 II, cols. 1257f;
cf. 1969, p.7). He likewise rejected a book which otherwise attracted
a great deal of attention when it appeared, namely Albert B. Lord's
The Singer of Tales (1960). Lord had collected materials among
tradents in the Balkans, and he was able to demonstrate that even if
the traditions were established by the oral speakers, something nevertheless occurred when they were fixed in written form. The materials
were imported into a new situation, and changes of emphasis and
transformations took place because the scribes were no longer subject
to the same controls on transmission as popular storytellers were.
Engnell rejected Lord's conclusions by pointing out that the words of
the prophets were not popular traditions; rather, the case of the OT
was unique, in that we here have to do with sacral-religious literature
which derived from a unified and special *Sitz im Leben.*

Engnell's protests did not reach the scholarly world at large. Already in 1959, when he lectured at the Old Testament congress at Oxford on "Methodological Aspects of Old Testament Study", Engnell
discovered that his views had little effect (Engnell 1960). This did not
necessarily mean so much at a congress at which many conservative
scholarly views predominated, but it does suggest that Lord's book
was to find a receptive audience when it appeared a year later.

Lord's assertion that the situation of traditional materials became
wholly changed by written fixation led scholars to question the value
of a traditio-historical research which relied on examination of the oral
tradition. Under such circumstances, one might ask, was it at all possible to get back to the oral tradition? This sort of scepticism made itself powerfully felt, and it has been thoroughly expressed by, for example, John Van Seters in his work on the Abraham traditions (1975).

In Germany the stress on oral tradition and the attendant rejection
of literary criticism simply made no headway. The type of traditio-historical research that characterized Scandinavian research was scepti-
cally received there, if they knew of it at all. Thus, when we hear of
tradition history in a German context, we should note that the concept has different content for German scholars. The German variety
was inaugurated by G. von Rad and M. Noth in the 1930's and was
concerned with the examination of large complexes of tradition. In

von Rad's case, tradition history had to do with the growth of the Pentateuch around an original nucleus consisting of an ancient and simple *credo* which continuously attracted other materials to it. Noth concentrated his interest on such diverse themes as the Exodus from Egypt, the Sinai traditions, the promises to the fathers, and so forth, which he held were ultimately joined together to form a larger work (von Rad 1938; Noth 1943 and 1948).

Since the point of departure for these scholars was the Pentateuch and the historical books, I shall not here attempt to account for this type of tradition history in greater detail. When German scholars discuss the books of the prophets, they prefer to speak of *Überlieferung* and *Überlieferungsgeschichte*. To give some impression of the relationship between this sort of traditio-historical study and the Scandinavian type, I shall now present a brief account of Hans Walter Wolff's commentary on the Book of Hosea, as it appeared in the *Biblischer Kommentar* (Wolff 1961). Following this, I shall offer a corresponding sketch of Ivan Engnell's understanding of Hosea, as depicted in *SBU* (Engnell 1962-63 I, cols. 978-987).

Wolff says nothing about oral tradition, but he begins by saying that it is virtually certain that some of the written tradition derives from Hosea himself, and in this connexion he refers to the first-person narrative in 3:1-5, which he believes belongs together with 2:4-17. He finds another hand (note the choice of expression) in 1:2-6.8f, which he assigns to a prophetic disciple. In 2:18-25 the disciple has reproduced a text which was presumably already fixed in written form. Thus Wolff arrives at his first independent complex of tradition, 1:2-6.8f, and 2:1-3:5. The other large complex of tradition embraces 4:1-11:11bβ. Here Wolff has rather greater difficulty explaining the context and the process of tradition, but he insists on a kerygmatic unity. The gulfs separating the various rhetorical units are in any case so large that Wolff is forced to include contributions or disturbances from the audience, and he even implies that the speaker had yet another faction among those present in mind, to whom he tailored his address (1961, p.xxv).

According to Wolff, the literary record of these passages was made by circles who followed Hosea, and who approved of his ideas, in contradistinction to the majority of the people. The third complex of tradition is ch.12-14, which Wolff regards as unlikely to derive from the prophet himself. The doxology at 12:6 shows that the complex was used in a cultic connexion in Judah.

Wolff further points to the close affinity between the Hoseanic traditions and the pre-Deuteronomistic movement, and he finds redactional additions stemming from the Deuteronomists. The author asserts that a glossator has also clarified individual oracles (2:10bβ; 4:9; 6:10b, etc.), and, finally, that a Judaean redactor has emphasized Judaean salvation-eschatology. Since some of the latter materials were inserted fairly early (1:7; 3:5), it is possible that the prophet may have directed his hopes towards Judah.

As one might expect, in his examination of the Book of Hosea Engnell renounces both a literary-critical view of the book and the presuppositions of such an approach. He states that one can not without more ado simply declare attacks on Judah to be additions, nor assurances of salvation or messianic passages. While it is true that we must assume a redaction in Jerusalem, it will have been the case already in the time of Hosea that it was felt that real salvation could be achieved by merely restoring the Davidic empire. Hosea himself may have shared this view. The mistakes of the past were to be corrected.

Engnell prefers to divide the book into four parts, 1-2; 3; 4-11; 12-14. He finds in the first part a description of a conscious prophetic symbolic action, the marriage with Gomer. The conclusion of ch.2 depicts Yahweh's new pact with Israel; Yahweh shows grace to the faithless, and the chapter ends on a hymnic-messianic note. It is obvious that, here as elsewhere Engnell uses the word "messianic" in an extended sense. Ch.3 deals with the same motifs and ends with a Davidic perspective: the people are to seek Yahweh, their God, and David, their king (3:5).

Like Wolff, Engnell is forced to go into detail in his discussion of the main section, chs.4-11. He designates the oracles as Israel-oracles, since they are addressed to Israel's children or to the house of Israel (mostly severe words of judgement). The well-known oracle at 6:1-3, concerning Yahweh who will arise on the third day, is interpreted by Engnell as a "šahid-verse", an Arabic term for a verse quotation, and in his opinion its frame of reference is a cultic scenario of death and resurrection. Ch.11 concludes on a positive expression concerning Yahweh's ability to forgive, and Engnell emphasizes that we have no reason whatsoever to deny this passage to Hosea.

The last part, chs.12-14, is introduced by an oracle against Ephraim, but Judah also receives sharp words of judgement. Finally, we encounter the hope that Israel will repent, and the assurance that a new time would then begin: "I will love them freely ... I will be as the dew to Israel".

Engnell stresses that the Book of Hosea is difficult to interpret. It is obvious that his interpretation of the book is guided by a comprehensive perspective which differs from Wolff's. It is equally clear that Wolff's understanding of Hosea is a direct continuation of the old literary-critical approach. The presuppositions of both scholars are present before they begin their exegesis.

In connexion with the view adumbrated above it is interesting to consider a third new treatment of the Book of Hosea, namely M.J. Buss' *The Prophetic Word of Hosea* (1969). Buss prefers to call his work a "morphological study", since he finds the designation "form-critical" too confining. Buss divides the book into three major parts. Chs.1-3 consist of three complexes which have a complicated oral prehistory. Already ch.1 is seen as encompassing two layers of tradition supplemented by later additions. 2:4 begins in juridical style with a "rib-pattern" address, and a number of additions follow subsequently. Ch.3 summarizes the foregoing, using ch.1 as its foundation, and it has also been expanded. The three complexes are held to have developed independently of each other, also after they were joined together.

Buss further holds that while the first three chapters developed orally over a long period of time, the subsequent chapters were written down at an early date, presumably as a memory aid, since here, too, the process of tradition will have been oral. Here there are few indications of secondary growth, just as the catchword associations are assumed to have been adopted from the oral tradition. In this connexion Buss, who, unlike the Germans, also reads the works of Scandinavian scholars, refers to Gerhardsson's *Memory and Manuscript* (1961).

Buss feels that there was a tendency to record curses in written form, which he asserts was the reason Hosea's pre-Exilic judgement oracles were written down and preserved in a permanent written tradition. He asserts that the two collections composed of chs.4-11 and 12-14 do not presuppose each other. Both begin with sections containing a *rib*, and both end on expressions of hope. As far as the "rib-pattern" speeches are otherwise concerned, I defer to Kirsten Nielsen's excellent study (1978).

Buss rejects Wolff's peculiar suggestion that chs.4-11 reflect an interplay between the prophet and his audience. He says that the tra-

dents may have been refugees from North Israel who reapplied the
threat and judgement oracles to Judah. The disconnected character of
the oracles which Wolff attempted to explain with the theory mentioned above is accounted for by Buss as an expression of an ecstatic
state. In this connexion Buss refers to Lindblom's observation that ecstatic states can produce disjunctive images and forms (Lindblom
1962, p.124); however, he also feels that there is more coherence in
these oracles than scholars usually are prepared to admit. The last
section, composed of chs.12-14, is held to be based on cultic oracles
and to constitute an ironic attack on the statements issuing from the
cult, while the conclusion goes off in another direction.

In his work Buss, who has briefly visited Scandinavia, makes use of
Nyberg, Mowinckel, Lindblom, and Gerhardsson, and he clearly
breaks with the literary-critical tradition, while in other matters going
his own way. Buss' rejection of the usual metrical schemes, which he
feels have little to do with the specific character of Hebrew poetry, is
also a break with literary criticism. As he says, the concept of a "verse
foot" can not be applied to Hebrew literature, unless by this one intends to signify a unit consisting of a "heavy" word, or a sentence
containing such a word. Each unit contains a naturally heavy accent;
in this sense, and, according to Buss, *only* in this sense, is it meaningful to speak of an accentuating rhythm.

The author further points out that Hosea is dependent upon existing traditions, which will have been perpetuated in both priestly and
prophetic circles. Hosea is held to presuppose an already-existing To-
rah tradition attached to Shechem; this tradition will probably have
included the fledgling beginnings of the Levitical idea as well as the
stream of conceptions which ultimately led to the composition of
Deuteronomy. Most of the metaphors and expressions employed by
Hosea were not new creations, but living symbols, even if they were
often given new applications or directions.

Buss' starting point was form-critical, but he ultimately found the
method too limiting in scope, perhaps owing to the influence of his
critical teacher, Millar Burrows of Yale. Thus his interest in Scandinavian research was awakened.

I have personally found Buss' work useful, especially in connexion
with my own book, *The Message of the Prophet Zephaniah* (Kapelrud
1975). My approach here was traditio-historical, though I included
aspects of other approaches to aid the elucidation of the text. In add-

ition to Buss I have discovered some interesting ideas in the *Anatomy of Criticism* of the Canadian literary scholar, Northrop Frye (1957). Frye's archetypal pattern is especially useful in the analysis of motifs in the prophetic books.

It is a natural and acknowledged fact that new impulses in research make themselves felt, and that scholars with dissimilar views learn from each other. Scholarship which is reluctant to revise and adjust its methods easily becomes dogmatic and thereby loses its character as research. However, new impulses are not always the same as influence; they can also function, as the poet Henrik Wergeland wrote, like "the insect's sting in the heart of the oyster", so that the result of a disagreeable impulse is a pearl. Poetical metaphor must not be taken too far, but Eduard Nielsen functioned as the "insect" of my metaphor when he wrote *Oral Tradition*. As mentioned above, Nielsen there considers the oral process by which Micah 4-5 were formed, where the individual units were joined together by catchword association (E. Nielsen 1954).

The French professor, B. Renaud of Strassbourg, was among the scholars who strongly objected to Nielsen's procedure, first in a book (Renaud 1964), and subsequently in his commentary on the Book of Micah, *La formation du livre de Michée* (1977). Renaud emphasizes that he has arrived at a radically different understanding of the redaction history of these two chapters from that proposed by Eduard Nielsen. Rather, instead of being an anonymous product created by happenstance, the chapters bear witness to a consciously organic structure, determined by a theological point of view. Renaud maintains that these sections were the handiwork of a Deutero-Micah, whose composition was an attempt at an eschatological-messianic synthesis intended to give hope to the sorely tried congregation in Jerusalem.

In the conclusion to his commentary, Renaud again mentions his relationship to Nielsen's views, but here it seems as if he attempts to modify his position and approach that of Nielsen. He does not feel that "la méthode dite 'traditio-historique' " has been completely successful with chs.4-5 (Renaud 1977, pp.421f), but he is not so dismissive when he discusses the way the book was assembled. Here he stresses that the various expressions will have been oral from the beginning, and that they may have been transmitted orally for a couple of centuries. Renaud feels that the confused state of Micah 1, with its lacunas and hopeless sentences, is only explicable as a result of oral tradition. On the other hand, he feels that the better preserved sections

2:1-4 and ch.3, which seem to be the prophet's own words, will probably have been transmitted in written form, as the text reveals no signs of oral transmission. Here, according to Renaud, the hypotheses of the Scandinavian school oversimplify matters. In this connexion he refers to an article of P. Grelot, who maintained that the sharp distinction between oral and written transmission is inappropriate to such formally well-defined materials as the prophetic texts (Grelot 1966). Indeed, one underestimates the Temple and palace scribes if one merely assigns practical matters to them, according to Grelot.

Renaud agrees with Grelot on this point, but in reality the idea is not foreign to the Scandinavian school, since already Engnell had maintained that the "liturgy type" of prophecy will have been written down at an early stage. Unfortunately, this conclusion was only presented in Swedish, and it is apparent that Renaud was unfamiliar with Engnell's work, while he makes frequent reference to Lindblom, Eduard Nielsen, and myself.

At this point I could, of course, continue and examine such recent studies as R.P. Carroll's *From Chaos to Covenant* (1981). Here the author makes use of motif-analysis, redactional study, and sociological analysis, while at the same time distancing himself from the commentaries on Jeremiah of, among others, Skinner (1922) and John Bright (1965). However, such an excursion would lead us too far afield, and, indeed, there is no need. We were previously able to note that already Engnell's concept of "traditio-historical prophetic study" in the 1940's and later was somewhat unclear and diffuse, but nevertheless necessary. His thesis suggested that it was a good idea to take one's point of departure in the oral tradition, and then attempt to pursue the tradition throughout its often complicated development. As already Engnell pointed out, and other scholars have subsequently stressed, it is necessary to use all possible approaches in a traditio-historical study. It is an "open" type of analysis, in which the scholar has not in advance committed himself to any particular views, as was often the case of scholars utilizing the old literary-critical method. This is not to say that the traditio-historical study of the prophets in Scandinavia has not also had a tendency to observe certain axioms, but this phenomenon is now a thing of the past. The methodological debate will no doubt continue, and new points of view will have their say, but the basic idea of traditio-historical research will persist. And exactly the fact that we have been able to provide new impulses has been our principal contribution to the study of the prophets.

ṣᵉdāqā IN THE SCANDINAVIAN AND GERMAN RESEARCH TRADITIONS

Bent Mogensen

Practically everyone translates *sedeq/ṣᵉdāqā* as "justice" and then immediately proceeds to add that the European concept of "justice" does not fully correspond with Heb. *ṣᵉdāqā*. One subsequently continues to translate the word as "justice", since it apparently is nevertheless the most suitable of the European words available. Thus it is probably not a bad idea to begin with a consideration of what *we* mean when we say "justice".

Justice is a socio-ethical concept; one is just in relation to others, that is, in relation to a community. Moreover, in the same way medical ethics have to do with a patient's health, so socio-ethics have to do with social health. As a rule, distribution is the main instrument of justice that is, of social health, in a society. In this fashion justice receives the meaning most often associated with it: equity. Social health and social equality are the connotations we Europeans have traditionally associated with the concept of "justice". The Romans have bequeathed us a concept of *justitia distributiva*, wherein equality is the main idea, and if one stresses the aspect of health, the Roman term is *justitia salutifera*, the justice that brings well-being. Superficially, it might seem as if there is a fundamental difference between the "blind" *justitia distributiva* and the "benevolent" *justitia salutifera*. However, as the Swiss socio-ethician Hans Ruh has noted (1981, pp. 67f), equality in and of itself is a formal concept which can not be allowed to remain purely formal; rather, it must be accorded a positive content in order to be meaningful. To create equality can only mean to improve the human situation; justice is to wish that my neighbour is as well off as I am. To wish that he is every bit as miserable as I is mere envy; this means that a *justitia distributiva* that is not also *justitia salutifera* is open to the destructive absurdities of envy. The

67

background of the often-heard demand for justice *can* be concern for the weak, but not infrequently this demand conceals the pettiness of envy within itself.

We also speak of justice when someone has transgressed against the community. In this event the community reacts by meting out a form of punishment which we evaluate as just or unjust, dependent upon whether or not we regard it as a suitable or unsuitable reciprocation for the transgression committed. In our human environment we tend to speak of and to act to achieve the resocialization of the transgressor, if his crime is the result of youth or other extenuation; that is, our practice directly and unequivocally expresses *justitia salutifera*. We look considerably more askance at the criminal who breaks the law for material gain; the narcotics pusher who faces six years in confinement is only getting his just deserts. Here an impartially retributive *justitia distributiva* takes precedence, and we can only speak of *justitia salutifera* in the sense that for a term of years society knows itself free of an unscrupulous parasite, and hopes that the severity of the example will reduce the numbers of such people even more.

And now to return to the question of "justice" in the Old Testament as illustrated by a selection of academic studies deriving from a number of times and places. Some of the not inconsiderable number of writers who have treated this subject indicate already in their titles that Heb. $s^e d\bar{a}q\bar{a}$ is not the same as European "justice". Thus K. Hj. Fahlgren's doctoral dissertation (1932) is called "$s^e d\bar{a}k\bar{a}$", and Klaus Koch's dissertation (1953) is called "sdq". Others denote the distance between the two concepts by bracketing "justice" with quotation marks, as here. A third group merely writes justice without more ado, and leaves the reader to discover for himself in the course of the book whether it offers an interpretation of Heb. $s^e d\bar{a}q\bar{a}$, or whether the author selectively discusses those texts which correspond to his European sense of "justice". A work which follows the latter course to a considerable extent is a product of the youth of the German Roman Catholic scholar Friedrich Nötscher, *Die Gerechtigkeit Gottes bei den vorexilischen Propheten* (1915). However, Nötscher quite reasonably took as his starting point a determination of the concept of $sedeq/s^e d\bar{a}q\bar{a}$ in which he battened on a definition offered by E. Kautzsch (1881): sdq means "norm-conformity" (*Normgemässheit*). Nötscher adds that such correspondence to a norm can express itself in the juridical, ethical or religious areas of life, and that it mainly expresses itself as an activity rather than as a trait of humour. As a juridical concept *sedeq/ṣeḏāqā* means in part legal procedure as such (Amos 5:7, 6:12), while in part it is a positive "justice", that is, an impartial exercise of the law (1915, pp. 4-6). The messianic king is said to exercise "justice" in the latter sense.

As an ethical concept *ṣeḏāqā* means "righteousness" (Nötscher 1915, p. 7), while as an ethico-religious concept it is best rendered by "piety", as in, for example, Zeph 2:3 (p. 9). Already at this point I should reveal that Nötscher strongly emphasizes the distributive-retributive character of OT "justice", and he accordingly has trouble accounting for a number of passages in the prophetic books in which the meaning of *ṣeḏāqā* very clearly tends in the direction of *justitia salutifera*, and in which such translations as "salvation" or "help" would be more appropriate (e.g. Jer 23:6). However, Nötscher asserts (p. 9) that *ṣeḏāqā* does not mean "salvation". Further, according to Nötscher, when Isa 1:27 says that Zion will be redeemed by justice, this refers to Yahweh's judgemental and punishing intervention which directly entails the destruction of his enemies and indirectly brings about the redemption of the pious. Yahweh in the theology of Isaiah and the other pre-exilic prophets is held to be the severe but just judge who weighs guilt and punishment, but who also spares those who are faithful to him. In this sense Yahweh is a *šōpēṭ ṣeḏeq* (Jer 11:20).

While the godless must fear Yahweh's *ṣeḏāqā* , the pious may rejoice in their fall. But is it true that we can only speak of *ṣeḏāqā* in this indirect and mediate way as *justitia salutifera*? This is actually his opinion, and if one would raise the objection against his view that in Micah 6:5 Yahweh's help and support to his people are called *ṣidqōt YHWH*, he replies that Israel had merited this aid – though how on earth he arrives at this conclusion is far from obvious! Also in the case of Micah 7:9 Nötscher concludes that justice is primarily retribution (1915, p. 27). After having defined *ṣeḏāqā* in this manner, that is, as in the main corresponding to a European-Roman Catholic *justitia distributiva*, a retributive principle, Nötscher pursues the "justice" thus construed in the works of the pre-exilic prophets, and the rest of his book has no bearing on our theme, since it no longer deals with *ṣeḏāqā* but with the relationship between guilt and punishment in the preaching of the pre-exilic prophets. Nötscher observes that this is a "completely balanced relationship" (*Verhältnis völliger Gleichheit*, p. 59), but that Yahweh makes appropriate allowances for the subjective

aspect of guilt and allows sins committed in ignorance to go unpunish-
ed. Here he especially finds support in Hos 4, which makes a negligent
priesthood responsible for the people's situation (pp. 50ff). Towards
the end of the book Nötscher compares the justice of Yahweh with
some of the other distinctive divine attributes and activities (pp. 93ff).
Yahweh's justice, as understood by Nötscher, is commensurate with
his "anger" and his holiness. The relationship between Yahweh's justice and his grace is, however, more controversial, and it is here abundantly clear that Nötscher's attempt to define $s^e d\bar{a}q\bar{a}$ onesidedly as *justitia distributiva* or *jus talionis* is difficult to maintain. The difficulties appear when $s^e d\bar{a}q\bar{a}$ appears together with *mišpāt*, as it often does,
and things go completely haywire when *mišpāt*, $s^e d\bar{a}q\bar{a}$, and *hesed* appear as largely synonymous concepts (Jer 9:23).

For those who have read Johs. Pedersen's *Israel* (1920) or read or
heard of Nelson Glueck's study of *hesed* (1928) which has led to the
victory of the interpretation of *hesed* as "covenant faithfulness",
Nötscher's difficulties in reconciling $s^e d\bar{a}q\bar{a}$ with *hesed* appear to be
of his own devising. But Nötscher understands *hesed* in the same way
as the Danish Bible translation of 1931 ("love", "grace", and "mer-
cy"), and since he has limited the concept of $s^e d\bar{a}q\bar{a}$ to punishing (retributive) justice, he encounters an antithesis which he is only able to
modify by seeking recourse to a typically theological evasion (Nötscher 1915, p. 104). He claims that Yahweh's justice aids the righteous by punishing sinners, so that there is no absolute contradiction
between justice and mercy (*hesed*). Again it is Micah 6:5 and 7:9
which make the harmony in Yahweh's nature problematical.

Nötscher's Yahweh is severe, but just. Two different pictures of
Yahweh's $s^e d\bar{a}q\bar{a}$ are painted by Emil Kautzsch in his previously-men-
tioned treatment (1881) and by L. Diestel (1860). Neither of these
works has been available to me, but one can make acquaintance with
them via Albrecht Ritschl's major dogmatic work, *Die christliche
Lehre von der Rechtfertigung und Versöhnung* in its second volume,
Der biblische Stoff der Lehre. Ritschl acknowledges his debt to
Diestel and Kautzsch in his analysis of $s^e d\bar{a}q\bar{a}$ (Ritschl 1900, p. 103).
We shall now – actually somewhat anachronistically – allow Ritschl
to take up the fight against Nötscher. As regards a provisional, purely
formal determination of $s^e d\bar{a}q\bar{a}$ as correspondence to a norm, there is
no disagreement between Nötscher and Ritschl. However, Ritschl
blankly denies that $s^e d\bar{a}q\bar{a}$ has anything to do with retributive justice

(p. 104); instead he holds that this notion could at most be applied to a very few passages, and even then only in post-exilic writings. Ritschl admits that Yahweh's *ṣᵉdāqā* is occasionally hard on the enemies of the deity and his people, and yet the goal of the activity designated *ṣᵉdāqā* is always the well-being of Yahweh's friends. Neutralization of the enemies is never an object in its own right; rather, it is always a means of preserving the lives of those who belong to Yahweh. Thus Ritschl sees no difficulty in the parallelization of *hesed* and *ṣᵉdāqā* in Ps 143:11f, since he there finds Yahweh's *ṣᵉdāqā* expressed in his rescuing activity, while Yahweh's annihilation of the enemies is said to result from his *hesed*.

Ritschl further points out that Yahweh is conceived of as lord of the whole world, so that one expects him to intervene punitively against evil men, and yet this side of Yahweh's activity is never directly associated with Yahweh's *ṣᵉdāqā*. To the contrary, Yahweh's *ṣᵉdāqā* is always directed towards "the just" (*saddīqīm*). An important argument against Nötscher's "punitive justice" is provided by Ps 69: 28f, where the poet asks Yahweh to exclude his enemies from Yahweh's *ṣᵉdāqā* . We may suppose that if *ṣᵉdāqā* really meant punitive justice, the poet would have requested that the enemies be allowed to taste it! Ritschl thus proposes a *ṣᵉdāqā* understood as *justitia salutifera* with the same zeal employed by Nötscher to characterize it as *justitia distributiva*. Ritschl sees *ṣᵉdāqā* understood as *justitia salutifera* to be exemplified in the writings of the poet he calls "the Babylonian Isaiah", Deutero-Isaiah (cf. Reiterer 1976). Nötscher's Yahweh is demanding, but just; Ritschl's Yahweh is both loving and firm.

We now turn our gaze upon Scandinavia, which is to say, upon Johs. Pedersen. One ought first to mention that Johs. Jacobsen, who was professor of Old Testament in Copenhagen from 1891 to 1929, and had been Johs. Pedersen's teacher, agreed with Ritschl's view in his theology of the Old Testament, as he says that in the OT we find "no antithesis between Yahweh's *sedeq, ṣᵉdāqā*, and his goodness or love; to the contrary, the one is subsumed under the other. Thus especially Deutero-Isaiah developed the concept of *sedeq*" (1917, p. 97).

Johs. Pedersen's views will be so well known that they may be summarized quite briefly: "The soul must be healthy in order to be able to develop in complete harmony; the Israelites term this sort of health 'justice' " (1920, p. 262; cf. Eng. p. 336). Thus Pedersen begins, and already here we detect that he is closer to Ritschl than to Nötscher.

Further, *justitia salutifera* is fully apparent in Pedersen's actual definition: "Justice is the spiritual attribute by means of which peace is
achieved" (p. 262). Against the notion of *justitia distributiva* he asserts that the Israelite's justice is not a "neutral, disinterested procedure of giving everyone his due round about". We should observe that
$\underset{.}{s}^e d\bar{a}q\bar{a}$ is defined as an attribute of the person, the "soul", and Johs.
Pedersen further characterizes this attribute as the will and ability, or
power, to act in accord with one's nature, to realize oneself. Yahweh's
justice is not different, it is merely unlimited. Thus "justice" is to
some extent self-assertive, but it is self-assertion within the framework
of the community within which the individual necessarily lives. Johs.
Pedersen calls this essential community among men the "covenant".
There is a covenant between relatives, friends, natives, and so forth;
thus justice is additionally also covenant-maintenance or observance.
It should be apparent that Johs. Pedersen's discussion of "covenant"
is not a religio-theological concept, but more a psychological and sociological category. We shall return to this shortly. It occurs to me
that Johs. Pedersen's discussion of "covenant" in conjunction with
$\underset{.}{s}^e d\bar{a}q\bar{a}$ has had an influence on subsequent research which he did not
intend and probably would not have accepted.

Johs. Pedersen's definition of $\underset{.}{s}^e d\bar{a}q\bar{a}$ applies to the classical use of
the concept in ancient Israel. But he regarded the picture of the dis-
solution of the old social harmony caused by urban life as described
by the prophets as the foundation of a development which made the
powerful unjust and the just too weak to secure justice for himself.
Thus the maintenance of justice is left to Yahweh, and a succesful
life is no longer the realization of justice, but a *reward* for justice performed by the powerless. This development is held to have culminated
in Judaism (1920, pp. 292f; cf. Eng. 376f). *Justitia distributiva* had
trouble taking over, and it got there late; the $\underset{.}{s}^e d\bar{a}q\bar{a}$ of Deutero-Isaiah
was unquestionably a *justitia salutifera* (p. 264; cf. Eng. p. 338), but
then, he was speaking of Yahweh's $\underset{.}{s}^e d\bar{a}q\bar{a}$, not man's.

We shall now attempt to follow Johs. Pedersen's conception of
$\underset{.}{s}^e d\bar{a}q\bar{a}$ through the realm of Scandinavian Biblical studies. Sigmund
Mowinckel did not hesitate to read *Israel I-II* so that Johs. Pedersen's
views are incorporated into his major work, *Psalmenstudien II* (1922).
Mowinckel here agrees with Pedersen's determination of $\underset{.}{s}^e d\bar{a}q\bar{a}$ as a
self-assertive and covenant-maintaining spiritual power (Mowinckel
1922, p. 70; p. 167). It is in the light of this concept that we are to

understand that activity of Yahweh which is designated $šāpaṭ$ ("to judge") in the Enthronement Psalms.

$Šāpaṭ$ is "ability/capacity to save" (*Heilstätigkeit*, 1922, p. 70). Like blessing, $s^e dāqā$ is seen as a quality inherent in man. Thus Mowinckel's understanding of $s^e dāqā$, as well as his use of the concept of covenant (*Bund*) closely corresponds to that of Johs. Pedersen.

K.Hj. Fahlgren's doctoral dissertation (1932) is a wide-ranging semantic study which deals with a considerable number of concepts which express solidarity or the opposite, among these being $s^e dāqā$. We find among the solidarity concepts *hesed*, which is in the main interpreted along the lines established by Nelson Glueck.

Johs. Pedersen's distinctive interpretation is also the natural point of departure for Fahlgren's study of $s^e dāqā$, although he does presume to correct the master a bit. Apparently Fahlgren finds Johs. Pedersen's expression, self-affirmation, too strong, for he says (Fahlgren 1932, p. 78) that Pedersen's understanding of $s^e dāqā$ is too individualistic in stressing self-affirmation and covenant-affirmation, thus giving preference to self-affirmation. Instead, Fahlgren feels, covenant-affirmation, that is, respect for the community, takes precedence. Here Fahlgren has not correctly understood Johs. Pedersen, for whom self-affirmation and covenant-affirmation were not two quantities, but one. Neither of them takes precedence, as they represent two sides of the same coin. As Pedersen says, "The soul always lives only in organic connexion with other souls, and it is only able to act in conjunction with others" (1920, p. 265; cf. Eng. p. 340). Outside of the covenant (the community) there is no life.

Fahlgren additionally disassociates himself from Johs. Pedersen by reducing the "power" Pedersen had attributed to $s^e dāqā$ to the more abstract "norm"; thus Fahlgren's definition of $s^e dāqā$ (1932, p. 82) is "norm of social intercourse" (*Norm des Gemeinschaftsverhältnisses*). Fahlgren deals briefly with the question of *justitia distributiva* versus *justitia salutifera* (pp. 99f); here he finds that Yahweh's $s^e dāqā$ is otherwise associated with hope and salvation. Ragnar Leivestad arrived at a similar conclusion a few years later (1946).

Up to this point $s^e d\bar{a}q\bar{a}$ had been understood as a quality (Johs. Pedersen's definition) inherent in Yahweh and in man. In recent decades the idea has appeared that $sedeq/s^e d\bar{a}q\bar{a}$ and related concepts were originally entities or personified forces. The first comprehensive treatment of this question was Helmer Ringgren's doctoral dissertation (1947). In the second edition of *Die Religion in Geschichte und Gegenwart* Mowinckel defines an hypostasis as a divine being which represents the personification of a quality or an activity of a superiour deity (1928, p. 8). A classical example of the concept is Egyptian *ma'at*, a powerful goddess who is celebrated in hymns (Ringgren 1947, pp. 45ff); her essence or field of operation is justice, or world order, as a more recent and better-considered expression puts it.

Among other hypostases discussed, Ringgren mentions the Babylonian pair of deities, Mešaru and Kettu (pp. 53ff). In this connexion Klaus Koch (1976, col. 509) mentions the word-pair *sedeq* and *mīšōr* which figure as royal qualities in Isa 11:4 and Ps 45:7f. Ringgren also regards it as probable that the cult of Ugarit knew a deity called *Sedeq* (1947, p. 82), while Johs. Pedersen (1941, pp. 66f) understands this *sedeq* as an attribute of KRT. From the Phoenician ambit we should note, as Ringgren says, that Philo of Biblos mentions the paired deities Misor and Sydyk in his *Phoinikika*.

In the Old Testament the two theophorous names Melchizedek and Adonizedek will be familiar; these two are associated with Jerusalem, which Isaiah (1:26) calls *'īr hassedeq*. Ringgren mentions as examples of hypostases in the Old Testament Ps 85:11-14, where *sedeq* and *šālōm* kiss each other, and where *sedeq* is in Yahweh's presence and, like him, looks down from heaven (Ringgren 1947, p. 86). The question, then, is whether this hypostasis is a poetic product, or whether it is a reminiscence of a deity called *Sedeq*. Ringgren believes the latter to be the case and subsequently offers the significant conjecture that a relationship will have obtained between El and *Sedeq* which corresponds to that which obtained between the sungod Re and Ma'at in Egypt (p. 87). In other words, *Sedeq* will have been an hypostasis of the supreme god, El.

Also of significance for later research is an observation of Aage Bentzen which Ringgren found in Bentzen's commentary to Ps 85: 11ff:

It is clear that 'faithfulness', 'truth', 'justice', and 'peace' are not human achievements, but divine gifts. This is the evangelical aspect of the psalm: happiness and goodness are awarded to those who turn their hearts to Yahweh (Bentzen 1939, p. 470).

This is ṣedeq's character of *justitia salutifera*, which Bentzen describes as an "evangelical aspect" in his last sentence; on the other hand, he also denies that ṣedeq *is* a divine name, although he leaves unanswered the question of what it might have been.

This is in contrast to Gösta Ahlström, who in his work on Ps 89 argues for a symbiosus between a Canaanite deity called Ṣedeq and Yahweh (1959, pp. 79ff). This symbiosus is held to provide the reason why ṣedeq/ṣᵉdāqā became one of Yahweh's more prominent attributes, the foundation of his throne, as we read in Ps 89:15 and Ps 97:2. Ahlström also finds the god Ṣedeq in the expression šaʿarē ṣedeq, "the gates of justice", in Ps 118:19 (p.80).

Ahlström battens on Johs. Pedersen in his definition of ṣedeq/ṣᵉdāqā when he says (Ahlström 1959, p. 81) that "ṣedeq, ṣᵉdāqā ordinarily designates something right, a quality of the soul, a relationship which has its centre, as far as religious and national affairs are concerned, in the covenant, bᵉrīt." This paraphrase of Johs. Pedersen's classical analysis of the concept is at once correct and slightly off the mark. It is correct that Johs. Pedersen speaks of the "covenant" as the sphere within which ṣᵉdāqā is confirmed. But when Johs. Pedersen says "covenant", he does not merely translate the Heb. bᵉrīt. As mentioned above, Pedersen regards the "covenant" as expressing the necessary fellowship among men; it is that covenant which is a feature of existence itself; bᵉrīt is merely one of the many forms this necessary fellowship may assume. Pedersen himself notes that bᵉrīt is most often used of a formalized fellowship, and that other designations for the covenant exist. Understood in terms of natural law, ṣᵉdāqā presupposes the covenant, but not necessarily bᵉrīt. Moreover, it is not by chance that Pedersen never mentions the word bᵉrīt in conjunction with ṣᵉdāqā, since these words practically *never* appear together in the Old Testament (cf. Koch 1976, col. 516). Johs. Pedersen's use of the word "covenant" in connexion with ṣᵉdāqā may be seen in a recent Danish work in systematic theology by Rudolph Arendt (1981). If I deliver my automobile to my local mechanic for a checkup, I do not enter into any sort of formal agreement with him as to the cost and duration of his service, and yet there is a covenant between us. He trusts me to pay my bill, while I entrust him with the task of ensuring that I may drive without fear of a breakdown.

Eduard Nielsen has written (1952, pp. 64f) that Scandinavian research has reason to be proud of the contributions of Mowinckel, Pedersen, and Fahlgren towards an understanding of $s^e d\bar{a}q\bar{a}$. I would agree on this point, and it is also correct that what makes an Israelite *saddîq*, "just", is his capacity to affirm his role within the community. But neither Pedersen, Fahlgren, nor Old Testament tradition would support Nielsen's view that Israelite $s^e d\bar{a}q\bar{a}$ probably became closely linked with a presumably originally Canaanite concept of $b^e rît$ on Canaanite soil. Moreover, Nielsen's definitive statement, that *"saddîq* is he who keeps the regulations of the covenant" is closer to a Jewish "legal positivistic" understanding of $s^e d\bar{a}q\bar{a}$ than it is to the classical Israelite variety.

As is well known, Johs. Pedersen's *Israel* was translated into English, and since the Germans read English, while the English do not read German, his views also penetrated into the German-speaking ambit. Emil Balla's article "Gerechtigkeit" (1928) is still undisturbed by Pedersen; Balla sees nothing creative in God's justice, but only his punishing or rewarding reaction to the good or evil deeds of men. Thus he agrees completely with Nötscher's then thirteen-year-old treatment. Nor does Johannes Hempel enter into dialogue with Pedersen concerning $s^e d\bar{a}q\bar{a}$ in his work of 1938. According to Hempel, the divine $s^e d\bar{a}q\bar{a}$ is *capable* of manifesting itself as "courtroom justice", *justitia distributiva*, but it primarily appears as "covenant faithfulness" (*Bundestreue*), *justitia salutifera*, as in the Song of Deborah, Jdg 5:11 and Micah 6:5. *Sedeq* and *hesed*, as he points out, go well together (Ps 103:6ff, cf. 1938, p. 159); both of them express the idea that Yahweh approves of and is faithful to those to whom he has attached himself (p. 156).

It is first with Klaus Koch's doctoral dissertation, *sdq im Alten Testament* (1953) that we meet a distinctively new interpretation of $s^e d\bar{a}q\bar{a}$. Of especial importance here is Koch's examination of $s^e d\bar{a}q\bar{a}$ as a *phenomenon*. Ringgren had already noted six years previously in his book (1947) (with which Koch was unfortunately unfamiliar, owing to conditions in postwar Germany) that $sedeq/s^e d\bar{a}q\bar{a}$ was something more than a quality inherent in Yahweh and in men. Under the influence of Artur Weiser's commentary on the psalms (1950), which strongly emphasizes the theophany as a cultic event, Koch attempts to show that Yahweh's *ṣedeq/ṣᵉdāqā* is regularly associated with the theophany (1953, p. 4), although he admits that this is not always a close association (p. 8).

But what is this *ṣᵉdāqā* whose arrival is announced together with that of Yahweh? Koch prefers not to call it an hypostasis, as already Mowinckel (1922, p. 284), followed by Ringgren, had done in his interpretation of Ps 85:11ff; rather, he designates *ṣᵉdāqā* as a "being", since it is undeniable that *ṣedeq/ṣᵉdāqā* has a degree of independent existence (Koch 1953, p. 15). By virtue of its association with the theophany event, this "being" is associated with the cult, and in particular with the festival which celebrated Yahweh's assumption of kingship, and which Mowinckel had dubbed the Enthronement Festival. On Koch's view, Yahweh comes to his people (the theophany motif) during this festival, and with him comes *ṣedeq/ṣᵉdāqā*, which is to say that *ṣedeq/ṣᵉdāqā* is a *gift* to man. As noted above, Bentzen suggests the same characterization in his commentary to Ps 85:11ff. (1939).

This aspect of *ṣᵉdāqā* as a gift is especially notable in two famous psalms. Ps 24:5 mentions the worshipper who receives blessing and *ṣᵉdāqā* from his God, while Ps 72:1 requests Yahweh to give the king *ṣᵉdāqā*. Thus, according to Koch, *ṣᵉdāqā* is neither an idea nor a quality, but a power which assists the people, as Amos (5:7 and 6:12) enables us to see (1953, pp. 30f). Further, Isa 1:21ff also reveals the independent power and range of *ṣᵉdāqā*; Yahweh's city will once again become a dwelling for *ṣᵉdāqā*. Koch admits that (p. 33) it is doubtful whether Ps 51:20 (*zibḥē ṣedeq*) can be taken to mean that the people receive their share of *ṣᵉdāqā* through sacrifice, but he points out that *ṣᵉdāqā* may also be regarded as a territory: in Ps 69:28 the worshippers pray that the enemy not be admitted to Yahweh's *ṣᵉdāqā* (p. 38). However, in several cases Koch is probably too prone to interpret *ṣᵉdāqā* with the preposition "b" locatively, whereas the instrumental or accompanying meaning is more likely to be dominant.

What is Koch's opinion of Johs. Pedersen? We may suppose that he does not agree with Pedersen that *ṣᵉdāqā* is a quality. He would say that while *ṣᵉdāqā* can express itself in self- and covenant-affirmation, it is not, as Pedersen thinks, a spiritual force in God and man that comes from within. Rather, *ṣᵉdāqā* is a divine force coming from without, a gift or sphere which man either participates in or not (Koch 1953, p. 41). The gift of *ṣᵉdāqā* is a gift which is also a demand. Thus Koch asserts that those who have received $s^e d\bar{a}q\bar{a}$ are to realize it and develop it through their own actions (pp. 41ff, 62). The one who does this is *ṣaddîq*, a word Koch renders as "faithful to the community" (*gemein-schaftstreu*); he does not say "covenant faithful" like Hempel, since he had probably even then made the discovery reflected twenty-five years later in his article on $s^e d\bar{a}q\bar{a}$ in THAT (1976, col. 516) that *ṣedeq/$s^e d\bar{a}q\bar{a}$* is only occasionally associated with $b^e r\bar{i}t$, which is, of course, the Hebrew word we associate with (Danish) "pagt", (Germ.) "Bund", and (Eng.) "covenant".

Koch regards the concept expressed by *ṣedeq/$s^e d\bar{a}q\bar{a}$* as an early inheritance from Canaan. It will presumably have been adopted together with the god-as-divine-king tradition, and he sees it as present already in the Song of Deborah, Jdg 5:11, which is therefore held to represent a Canaanized Yahweh religion (1953, pp. 64f).

Klaus Koch has determined the concept of $s^e d\bar{a}q\bar{a}$ phenomenologically as a divine gift mediated through the cult, which is the life-giving centre. In so doing he follows his master, Gerhard von Rad (1950, p. 426f). In terms of content Koch defines $s^e d\bar{a}q\bar{a}$ as "faithfulness to the community" (*Gemeinschaftstreue*). The question is, what community? Johs. Pedersen would reply that it is that fellowship which *must* obtain between man and man and between God and man; it is this necessary community which Pedersen calls the "covenant". Now, a number of scholars have seized on this term, which was intended in the sense of a natural-law-concept by Pedersen, and they have employed it of the Covenant par excellence, the covenant on Sinai between Yahweh and Israel.

In recent German Biblical scholarship this misunderstanding of Johs. Pedersen has been combined with the famous amphictyony theory in such a way that $s^e d\bar{a}q\bar{a}$ sometimes receives an "amphictyonic" content. Thus $s^e d\bar{a}q\bar{a}$ is an element of the covenantal fellowship; this fellowship is the Israelite amphictyony; $s^e d\bar{a}q\bar{a}$ here designates the legal provisions of the amphictyony, which we encounter in the apodictically formulated laws. Has Johs. Pedersen unintentionally contributed to this neo-orthodox legal-positivistic concretion of $s^e d\bar{a}q\bar{a}$? This reinterpretation was signalled by Gerhard von Rad (1950, p. 423), who held that the fellowship to which $s^e d\bar{a}q\bar{a}$ applies is Yahweh's covenantal community with Israel, where $s^e d\bar{a}q\bar{a}$ consists in keeping the cultic and legal provisions of the Covenant.

This legal-positivistic "amphictyonic" understanding of *ṣᵉdāqā* may be further illustrated by a few examples. In Hans Walter Wolff's work on Hosea (1953), *da'at ᵉlōhīm* is, among other things, knowledge of concrete regulations ordained by Yahweh, so that *ṣᵉdāqā* is translated in Hos 2:21 and 10:12 as "covenant law". Similarly, Richard Hentschke understands Jer 23:5f to imply that a king after God's own heart will be a "theocratic functionary whose job is to maintain the sacral covenant law" (1957, p.31). Just because the king maintains *mišpāṭ* and *ṣᵉdāqā* in the land! In an analogous spirit Walter Beyerlin interprets *ṣidqōt YHWH* in Micah 6:5 as Yahweh's fulfilment of his covenantal obligations (1959, p. 73). While always conceivable, this is not in the text.

In defense of von Rad we ought perhaps to mention in connexion with his interpretation of *ṣᵉdāqā* that he later acknowledges (1957, p. 373) that concrete regulations only comprise a part of the more extensive *ṣᵉdāqā* with which Yahweh will allow Israel to be filled. Here von Rad draws on the conclusions of his talented pupil (Klaus Koch), and emphasizes the character of *ṣᵉdāqā* as divine gift and happiness-creating field of power (p. 374). Von Rad further praises Johs. Pedersen for having liberated the idea of *ṣᵉdāqā* from its foreign, European, characteristics, but he also agrees with Klaus Koch's critical objections: *ṣᵉdāqā* does not originate in the personality, *nepeš*, as Pedersen holds.

"Norm-conformity" (Kautzsch) and "community-faithfulness" (Koch) are attempts to find a Germanic word which catches the nature of *ṣᵉdāqā*. A more recent effort in this direction has been made by H.H. Schmid (1968), who describes *ṣᵉdāqā* as "world order" (*Weltordnung*), analogous to Egyptian *ma'at*. Schmid holds that the social category "community-faithfulness" does not cover the whole semantic range of *ṣᵉdāqā*; it does not include the cult, nor the areas of nature and fertility. However, Schmid maintains, the concept of "world order" encompasses the ethical, the cultic, and the "natural". I should like to add that this "ordering" viewpoint was not unknown to earlier scholars. The comparison with Egyptian *ma'at* was already mentioned by Ringgren (1963, p. 119), just as Gerhard von Rad had spoken of Yahweh's "will to order" (*Ordnungswille*) (1957, p. 372), and in his commentary on the psalms Artur Weiser not infrequently renders the concept of *ṣᵉdāqā* with the word "order" (*Ordnung*); see 1950, pp. 424, 436f, 463, etc.).

An examination of the concept of $s^e d\bar{a}q\bar{a}$ in Scandinavian and German scholarship remains primarily, as we have seen, a study of the reception of Johs. Pedersen's contribution to the understanding of the term. In this connexion Gerhard von Rad's evaluation in *Theologie des Alten Testaments I* is quite accurate: Johs. Pedersen's interpretation has provided a shield to the Israelite spiritual realm against the importation of European ideals. Furthermore, Johs. Pedersen's analysis of the concept has unquestionably contributed to the victory of the *justitia salutifera* view over the previously fairly prominent *justitia distributiva* concept. However, Pedersen's localization of the $s^e d\bar{a}q\bar{a}$-force within the individual self-affirming personality (or "soul") has been less accepted on German soil, and it has had to give way to interpretations of a less psychological and more theocentric nature.

TRADITION AND HISTORY, WITH EMPHASIS ON THE COMPOSITION OF THE BOOK OF JOSHUA

Magnus Ottosson

Swedish traditio-historical research has long been dominated by the name of Ivan Engnell. During the whole of his fruitful period as, first, lecturer and, subsequently, professor at the theological faculty at Uppsala, Engnell strove to inaugurate and refine a method designed to crush classical literary criticism and its attendant continuous-source hypothesis, which he felt required an "anachronistic and modernly bookish" understanding of the Old Testament. Engnell's lectures and writings comprised a gigantic, frequently elegant and ironic break with literary criticism. By way of contrast, he painted an engaging picture of the study of the text based on the MT. Engnell sketches out in ten points the only "legitimate" way of proceeding in his article "traditionshistorisk metod" (1962-63 II, cols. 1254-61)[1].

Here it appears that the principal task of an exegete approaching a text is to work out a compositional or formal analysis of it. This entails the uncovering of traditional works, collections of traditions, complexes of traditions, the isolating of individual units of tradition, as well as the identification of strata within an oral tradition. Such analysis requires one to pose all manner of questions as to form, content, principal motif, Tendenz, and technique of tradition; it should never be pushed to the point where one ignores the requirement of synthesis, that is, the interpretation of the relationship of lesser units to their context.

The relationship between oral and written tradition has long composed an area of interest for the Scandinavian traditio-historical school. It was important to Engnell that one *not* attempt to oppose the various types of tradition to each other. Large complexes of tradition may have existed orally at an early stage, prior to the written fixation of traditions; but this written fixation of the materials will not have brought them anything new, since, according to Engnell, oral tradition was extremely reliable; it was able to preserve both the authenticity and the integrity of traditional materials.

The ultimate task of text criticism was confined to *recensio* in a broad sense, that is, to the reconstruction of the MT.

This is a very short summary of those cardinal points which formed the basis for the "correct" use of traditio-historical method. As one of Engnell's former pupils it has been a matter of course for me to attempt to follow up Engnell's methodological initiatives. Although I can not accept all of Engnell's conclusions, it is nevertheless striking to note that even in cases where Engnell was not able to carry out an analysis in detail, he nevertheless had a discriminating feel for the organization of motifs and context of the texts[2].

It must be accounted presumptuous to claim that a traditio-historical method drawn in such simple categories could be able to threaten the literary-critical school which totally dominated then-contemporary exegesis. The issues of Engnell's programme express a reaction to the exaggerated literary criticism which reigned in the nineteen twenties and thirties[3]; moreover, it is probable that Uppsala's isolation during the Second World War also contributed to a certain exclusiveness in matters of method and basic attitude.

The traditio-historical Panorama:

What strikes one on reading literary-critical commentaries and analytical works is the formulaic assortment of value judgements one encounters in the course of analysis, phrases such as "addition, secondary addition, later gloss, expansion," and so forth. The reason seems to be that scholars attempt to reduce a text by analysis to yield an original nucleus which has been the object of a number of "redactions". As a rule, one finds no general agreement as to the time, or indeed the reason for the occurrence of such changes in a text. The reason for this is most often the fact that the text is divided up differently by different exegetes. According to Engnell, corroboration for the assumption of secondary expansion is lacking, and the traditions will have achieved significant form already at the oral level[4].

If we keep to the historical books, Engnell had presupposed a half caesura in the evolution of the texts. A "P Work" consisting of the first four of the Books of Moses existed, plus a "D Work" consisting of Deut-2 Kgs. A Chronistic Historical Work, dependent to a large extent on the "D Work", will have existed in the last stage. The relationship between the "P Work" and the "D Work" was cautiously described by Engnell:

> It is ultimately unlikely that we shall be able to decide the question of the temporal relation between 'P' and 'D', that is, between the 'Tetrateuch' and the 'Deuteronomistic Historical Work'. In both cases we are in the time of Ezra and Nehemiah, and we might just as easily say merely that they are 'different' from each other (among other things, the one represents Southern and the other Northern tradition) and that the 'Tetrateuch', generally speaking, contains far more older material than does 'D' (Engnell 1945, p. 231)[5].

Already in his early writing, Engnell emphasized that there was no Deuteronomistic material in the "P Work", nor any P material in the "D Work" (p. 203). Similar views recur in the works of M.Noth[6]. In his last article on the subject Engnell (1962-63 II, cols. 158f) very clearly characterized "P" as the circle of traditionists who passed on the "P Work" or Tetrateuch to posterity. Within this circle of tradition the ancient materials survived in both written and oral form; however, these materials can not be disclosed by source-critical analysis, although they may be differentiated form-critically. In its final form the "P group" belongs in Jerusalem, but it has roots extending to Hebron and Kadesh-barnea and thus represents a cluster of southern traditions. A notable characteristic of this group is its prominent antiquarian interests which, among other things, have resulted in the preservation of historical material in genealogical form. The group is further interested in cult and ritual; sacral institutions, and especially the Temple are always central. In spite of these aspects it is difficult to think of the group as simply composed of priests; rather, there is more of a flavour of the office of the royal antiquary. The attitude evinced towards the materials preserved by the tradition is broadminded and affirmative, just as their further tradition is faithful.

The centre is comprised of the Passover Festival, followed by Moses. The centralization of the cult to Jerusalem is nowhere acknowledged in "P"; this fact attests the antiquity of the tradition, a fact also supported by the occurrence of archaisms and the prescriptions of the Festival Calendar. The tradition of the Feast of Tabernacles no doubt dates from pre-Jerusalemite times. The legal materials also bear witness to great antiquity. The date of the activity of the P group must be set rather late, in late Exilic or post-Exilic times; this implies that the final form of the "P Work" was contemporary with the "D Work", or perhaps slightly older.

Engnell maintained that in practice the "P Work" and "D Work" were two large, unrelated collections of tradition which were most likely joined together by the Deuteronomist: "And although no trace of the Deuteronomist's revision is to be found within the "P Work", this alternative is in the nature of things to be preferred as the most natural and plausible" (1962-63 II, col. 161).

In terms of formal-literary factors and considerations of content, the Deuteronomistic Historical Work is more comprehensive than is the "P Work". For it was the Deuteronomist whose perspective was systematic; it was he who depicted the course of history schematically according to the device of Fall, Punishment, Repentance, and Salvation. He allows his own ideology to speak in long speeches and inclusio-narratives, which also permit his transmitted materials to speak. The Deuteronomist is anti-royalist and proclerical; the centralization of all cult to Jerusalem is his great ideological theme, and he regards all cult outside of Jerusalem with contempt. Now and again the Deuteronomist gives a feeling of being a real author or "school" of authors (Engnell 1945, pp. 231f).

The points so schematically listed above offer a compressed comparison of the characteristics of the two historical works, according to Engnell. Engnell himself never had opportunity to examine his theses in detail; nevertheless, these insights, comprising as they do Engnell's traditio-historical last will and testament, are a rich trove for future exegetes. In what follows we shall see that I do not slavishly follow my old teacher, but I do regard the basic idea of a "P Work" and a "D Work" as realistic. To this it is necessary to add that the P traditions are not merely limited to the "P Work", since P structures are often discernible in archaic form in the Book of Joshua as well.

The Relationship between "P" and "D":

There is much to be gained from the reconstruction of these two long-completed traditional works, that is, including the "P Work". In this way, one achieves a reasonably assured point of departure for contextual analysis. The junctures between the two works that were effectuated by the Deuteronomist are not supposed to have introduced revolutionary changes. According to Engnell, only the concluding narrative in the "P Work", the account of the death of Moses, will have been omitted. The two traditional works will have been the historical books of their respective circles, with different chronologies and different understandings of saving history. According to Engnell, these works also came into being independently of each other; thus there is not supposed to be any Deuteronomistic material in the "P Work", nor any "P material" in the "D Work".

Extremely few contemporary exegetes would dare be so categorical in their pronouncements in this respect. It is difficult to avert one's gaze from those texts in the "P Work" which nevertheless recall Deuteronomistic style. Moreover, their contents are such that, had they been located in the "D Work" we should naturally have pronounced them Deuteronomistic. Here one naturally thinks of such texts as Gen 14 (Astour 1966), Exod 32 (in which v. 7-14 are regarded as a Deuteronomistic addition, cf. Noth 1972, p. 271), and several long sections in Num (Noth 1943, p. 247). This sort of question can be attacked rather easily by concordance studies of expressions and phrases. Such a procedure, however, would be insufficient in and of itself, as one must also undertake an analysis of the context. Contextual analysis readily shows that one does not need to hypothecate the hand of a Deuteronomistic glossator in the P Work; rather, one could as easily argue that the (P) tradent had employed a traditional language to underline certain important motifs. For example, Gen 12-15 are so composed that their various motifs correspond to the Deuteronomistic understanding of the land, and yet these chapters are not rooted in a Deuteronomistic context. It can be shown that Dtr made use of these or similar materials in constructing his conception of the land in, e.g., the Book of Joshua. In so doing, he begins in Jos 1 with the same enormous area that recurs in Gen 15:18, which, however, is decimated (no doubt because of failure to observe the Law) in accordance with Gen 14-13 (in this order), in order ultimately to legitimate the later area by means of the "Landtag" at Shechem in Jos 24/Gen 12:6. Compare in this connexion the following progression in Deut: 1:7f.; 11:24; 34:1ff. The "P group's" traditional delimitation of the land, that is, Canaan, is discernible in Gen 10:19, can be glimpsed in Jos 22:19, and ;curs in Ezek 48, where all the tribes are somewhat high-handedly located west of the Jordan. Of course, this description played no political role in Israelite history; Israel burst the borders of Canaan by laying claim to the lands to the east of the Jordan. These claims were legitimated in turn by the accounts of the wanderings of the patriarchs and their struggles with elements of the Amorite population. Such collection and preservation of tradition was the major contribution of the P tradents to Israelite historical writing. The composition of these traditions was surely intuitively linked to the known course of historical development; therefore the full extent of David's kingdom was assumed to apply to the time of the patriarchs (Pedersen 1920, p. 22). It would thus be incorrect to ascribe any role to the Deuteronomist in the P traditions mentioned above, and correct to assert the lack of Deuteronomistic influence on the P texts.

But is there any P material in the "D Work"? Engnell denied this, and the few literary critics who have disagreed with him have claimed that the P fragments observable in Deuteronomistic texts must derive from a late post-Exilic glossator (Noth 1953, pp. 10f.). Accordingly, P supplements have been regarded as quite without interest. Nevertheless, one should enquire as to why they are present in the "D Work" at all. The literary-critical explanation of these passages appears all too simple; it might even be the case that they provide important clues to an understanding of Deuteronomistic ideology.

In the Book of Joshua it is not difficult to sort out P structures with a particular pattern and vocabulary stock corresponding to sections in the "P Work", and, indeed, J. Blenkinsopp has recently called attention to the numerous P characteristics which are to be found in the Book of Joshua (1976, pp 287ff). According to Blenkinsopp, P's main concern in connexion with the land is not so much its conquest as the establishment of a legitimate cult in it. Concentration on cultic legitimacy is otherwise a Deuteronomistic trademark, and I believe it is prominent in the composition of the Book of Joshua in, for example, the striking disinterest in matters that have to do with the Northern Kingdom. Furthermore, the cultic P references in the Book of Joshua seem to be intended to elevate Joshua to Moses' stature; more on this in the following.

Blenkinsopp does not deal more extensively with the relationship between P and D in Joshua, but since his understanding of P is the traditional literary-critical variety, he would probably assert that the

P structures in Joshua are later than the Deuteronomistic redaction (Dtr). In what follows, however, I shall attempt to demonstrate that the P structures in Joshua are only meaningful if they are seen in conjunction with the Deuteronomistic composition. In connexion with the texts, precise concordance studies may be able to suggest the origins and background of various phrases and formulas, but these observations are insufficient if one does not manage to penetrate to the intention underlying the composition. I shall here pursue three possible pathways to revealing an internal connexion between P and D[7]. Furthermore, I do not hesitate to suggest that Dtr knew certain P traditions in the form in which they are present in the so-called "P Work" and employed them in the composition of the Book of Joshua. The body of texts I find most appropriate in this connexion are Jos 3:1-8:35. In further corroboration of my thesis I would cite the idealized conception of the land in the Book of Joshua and its relation to the geography of the Abraham traditions; and, finally, I shall offer a comparison between the understanding of history entertained by "P" and Dtr.

I. Joshua 3:1-8:35

Joshua 3-6 has a clearly liturgical character exemplified by the convoluted "procession" leading to Gilgal and the subsequent wanderings round about Jericho. The Ark of the Covenant occupies the centre of the stage in these proceedings. Although the choice of language and phraseology in these materials is foreign to the Deuteronomistic vocabulary, it is nevertheless clear that the segment is a Deuteronomistic composition which contains liturgical materials attached to the cult site at Gilgal. A number of motifs in the description of the passage over the Jordan are reminiscent of the episode at the Sea of Reeds, to which the catechetical explanation at 4:23 also refers (cf. Norin 1977, pp. 35.40f.). P phraseology has been well incorporated into the text. Jos 7 is an independent section without visible signs of Deuteronomistic reworking. The archaic style of P dominates throughout the chapter, in which Joshua additionally functions in a peculiar capacity as intercessor after the failure of the attack on the city of Ai[8]. Ch. 8 is Deuteronomistic, and the episode dealing with the construction of the altar on Mt. Ebal, 8:30-35, is a Deuteronomistic reworking of old traditional material (E. Nielsen 1955, pp. 76ff.295ff)[9]. In these pages, the siglum "P" stands for the traditional material which is also to be found in the Tetrateuch, the "P Work". The occurrence of the P style in the following sections strongly implies that the traditions in question must derive from priestly circles attached to the shrine at Gilgal. I shall now attempt to point to some examples suggestive of a significant P dominance in Jos 3-8.

Ch. 3. "And N.N. rose early in the morning" is an expression that follows close on a nightly divine oracle in such P texts as, e.g., Exod 24:4. The situation is the same in Jos 3:1; 6:12; 7:16. Jos 8:10, however, is Deuteronomistic. There are clear signs of Deuteronomistic formulation in Jos 3:2-4, since Levitical priests figure here as the bearers of the Ark; cf. Deut 10:8; 31:9. 25f; Jos 8:33. It is difficult to determine just what we should make of the instruction to remain "two thousand cubits" from the Ark in v. 4. It is conceivable that the instruction is related to the measurement of the extent of the uplands of the Levitical cities in Num 35:5; that is, it is a figure associated with the Levites in v. 3 and combined with their role as bearers of the Ark of the Covenant. In consideration of contents and word choice, Jos 3:5 is obviously not Deuteronomistic. The injunction to sanctification as a prelude to witnessing Yahweh's activity figures in such P texts as Exod 19:10.14 and Num 11:18; cf. Jos 7:13. In the "D Work" the term *niplā'ōt* ("wonders") is only attested in Jdg 6:13, but recurs frequently in the Psaltar (note, however, the occurrences at Exod 34:10 and Exod 3:20 — wonders in the midst of Egypt).

Jos 3:7 opens on a typically Deuteronomistic note, "This day I will begin to exalt you in the sight of all Israel" (see also Jos 4:14). The same construction recurs in Deut 2:25 by way of introduction to the Amorite wars east of the Jordan (cf. Deut 2:24.31). The continuation of this chapter is clearly Deuteronomistic; see, for example, in v. 9-10 the enumeration of the *seven* peoples. A number of phrases and expressions in the chapter, such as the motions of the waters of the river, could tend to suggest an inherited vocabulary presumably deriving from liturgical traditions of a P type.

The geographical notice in v. 16 is unclear. "Adam" is thought to have been an important fortress guarding the ford leading to the interior of North Israel via the *wādī el fārʿa*; the notice recording that the Jordan was only dry in its southern reaches may thus have a southern provenance.

Ch. 4 is partially dominated by the somewhat complicated procedure according to which twelve men are deputed to fetch stones from the bottom of the Jordan, at the point where the priests bearing the Ark of the Covenant stand, in order to place them (*hinnīaḥ*) at the overnight campsite. In place of these stones, Joshua commands that twelve others be erected (*hēqīm*) in the middle of the river (v. 9). The previously-mentioned stones are subsequently erected (*hēqīm*) in Gilgal (v. 20). Both of Joshua's procedures here are accompanied by parallel catechetical explanations (v. 6 and 21ff, respectively). The stones which were placed in the river are said to be there "to this day" (cf. 4:7), but not the stones in Gilgal. We may suppose that we have here to do with a "censored" aetiology for the name Gilgal (= ring of stones, cf. Jdg 3:19.26). The Deuteronomist connects the name with the rite of circumcision at Jos 5:9.

The motifs present in Jos 4 have much in common with P material. Direct reference is made to the events at the Sea of Reeds in v. 23, and the crossing of the Jordan is dated according to the dating-scheme of P in v. 19 (cf. Wilcoxen 1968). The crossing of the East Jordanian tribes over the Jordan "before Yahweh" is here recorded in the same fashion as in Num 32:27, cf. Deut 1:18 and Jos 1:14, which has the expression "before your brethren".

The two catechetical explanations of the stones in the Jordan and at Gilgal, respectively, are most closely approximated by the celebration of the Passover at the Sea of Reeds in Exod 12:26f. The Deuteronomist has Joshua elevated to equality with Moses. Moses places twelve pillars at the foot of Mt. Sinai (Exod 24:4) in conjunction with the covenant ritual. However, the Deuteronomist uses *'abānīm*, since the P expression, *maṣṣēbā*, employed in Exod 24, will have been too ideologically "loaded" a term.

Ch. 5 contains accounts of the circumcision and celebration of the *pesaḥ maṣṣōt*. The name "Gilgal" is derived from the verb *gālal*, "to roll", an etymology of assuredly redactional character and somewhat on the order of a play on words. The connexion of this chapter with the P materials is quite clear. The promise to the fathers, among other passages adumbrated in Gen 17:8-14, is recapitulated, and circumcision is again the sign of the covenant, v. 10. No uncircumcised persons were permitted to celebrate the Passover in Exod 12:44.48, and the festival was to be celebrated on arrival in Canaan according to Exod 13:5. The expression *šēnīt*, "a second time" (v. 2), should be

taken to imply that the rite of circumcision prior to the Passover celebrated in Egypt was understood as undertaken in unison. Ch. 5:13-15
is associated with P material by reason of the parallelism between v.
15 and Exod 3:5; here v. 15 may for practical purposes be described
as a "quotation" by the Deuteronomist in the interests of elevating
Joshua to Moses' peer, whereby the deity is transformed into the com-
mander of Yahweh's army. It is possible to regard this section as a
follow-up of Exod 23:20ff, which belongs to the Sinai traditions;
cf. Exod 24:4; Jos 4:20[10].

The co-incidence of circumcision and Passover Festival at the point
directly after the crossing of the Jordan must have been ideologically
motivated; it is presumably intended to emphasize Israel's distinc-
tiveness from the Canaanite population. Indeed, the two events may
be intended to represent the fulfillment of the obligation in Exod
13:5, that is, the stress on prompt compliance precisely "*when* Yahweh brings you into the land". A similar charge is present in Deut
27:2; this admonition *may* have prompted the notion of Joshua's
stones at Gilgal (cf. Deut 11:30). In this connexion we should also
recall that, according to the P traditions, the area east of the Jordan
was "unclean land" (Jos 22:19).

Ch. 6. Without undertaking a close analysis of the chapter dealing
with the fall of Jericho, it is sufficient to note that it is commonly
recognized that the people's circuits round about the city reflect a
liturgical procession rather than a military procedure. In conjunction
with this we read of *ḥẹrem* regulations of the most horrible sort;
all life in the city, "both men and women, young and old, oxen,
sheep, and asses" (6:21), are to be eradicated, just as all booty is to
be burnt and all metal objects are to be deposited in the house of Yahweh (v. 19.24) (Lohfink 1978). This notion involves such prodigious
destruction that it agrees very poorly with Deuteronomistic thought;
the latter appears in Jos 8:2, where the Israelites are permitted to des-
poil, among other things, livestock. Jos 7 still deals with the non-Deuteronomistic *ḥẹrem* regulations; we shall return to this point shortly,
but here it is enough to note that the draconic form was attached to
the sanctuary at Gilgal, as 1 Sam 15 indicates. Only the conclusion of
Jos 6 bears the imprint of Deuteronomistic style in the notice on the
treatment of Rahab.

The Ark of the Covenant plays a conspicuous part in the procession around Jericho; its role here was possibly understood as the cul-

mination of the passage over the Jordan. Yahweh's power is manifested via the use of the processional verbs *sābab* and *nāqap* (Ps 48:13; 47:6; Neh 12:31), which figure distinctively in 1 Sam 5, and not least in 1 Chr 13:3, during the transportation of the Ark from Kiriath-jearim to Jerusalem. If one takes the liturgical interpretation of Jos 6 seriously, it is an obvious step to connect the chapter with the Gilgal materials. In the preceding pages we have noted the abundance of P passages in the chapters under discussion, so it is only logical to assume that they were at home in Gilgal, where they will have been preserved in priestly circles.

Jos 7 will assuredly have belonged to the same circle of tradition as that responsible for the account of the consecration of Jericho to destruction. Achan's sin is defined as the theft of goods belonging to Yahweh, which is to say that they are *ḥērem* (Note the keyword *'ākar* in Jos 6:18; 7:25). This type of sin is more closely specified as *ma'al*, "breach of covenant", in Jos 7:1.11. The unity of the chapter can hardly be doubted, though the aetiology at the end of the chapter could be questioned as a redactional addition. Moreover, Deuteronomistic language and style are fully absent, while a number of expressions are reminiscent of P's style; this is especially true of v. 2-9. M. Noth assigns the chapter to the Gilgal materials (1953, p. 12), although he does not remark on the P style. However, one should compare the chapter with Num 14:2f; 20:3ff; Exod 17:3; Num 11:20 (Joshua is mentioned in Num 11:28), and Num 21:5. Furthermore, Joshua performs Moses' classical intercessory role here; cf. Exod 32:31ff. Jos 7 contains the spectrum of possible breaches of covenant, from hybris in v. 3 to more prosaic features in v. 11f. This register of sins was six-fold according to an original reckoning in v. 10-12. Everyone is under suspicion until the individual responsible is "taken" by lot in v. 14f, and punished in v. 24. Thus the same draconic principle is applied here as in Jos 6. Joshua takes Achan, the silver, mantle, bar of gold, his sons and daughters, oxen, asses, sheep, and all of his other possessions and stones and burns them with fire. In short, the same principle of consecration to destruction characterizes both Jos 6 and 7. Although the chapter is not Deuteronomistic, the account of the defeat at Ai is of great importance for the Deuteronomist's composition.

Ch. 8 contains namely the account of the victorious attack on Ai: for the first time in the Old Testament we are told of tactical manoeuvres in connexion with combat. The tactic in question is a simple ambush. Following the defeat of the enemy, however, we read of devastation according to the Deuteronomistic pattern. In 8:25 we read that 12,000 were killed, "both men and women", but v. 27 adds "Only the cattle and the spoil of that city Israel took as their booty, according to the word of Yahweh which he commanded Joshua" (cf. 8:2). Joshua subsequently constructs an altar on Mt. Ebal, according to the rules of the game, where he engraves on the stones there a copy of the Law of Moses. The Ark of the Covenant is present, and the blessing and curse formulas are pronounced from Mts. Garizim and Ebal, respectively, as prescribed by Deut 27.

The command to construct an altar on Mt. Ebal directly after the victory at Ai simply must be regarded as a peculiarity by anyone who is even slightly familiar with the geography of Palestine. The section at 8:30-35, however, is transparently Deuteronomistic and is no doubt to be assigned to Dtr. In terms of contents, choice of words, and structure it is dependent on Deut 11:26-30 and Deut 27:4ff. The reasons for locating the section immediately after the successful campaign against Ai are, however, difficult to discover. M. Noth (1953, ad loc.) felt the reason to be that the way to Shechem lay open after the victory at Ai. But since the section has nothing to do with what precedes and follows it, J.A. Soggin (1972, ad loc.) holds that it is to be relocated to follow Jos 24:27. Here the LXX is instructive, since it places the passage after Jos 9:2. However, there must have been some reason for locating the section precisely here. Personally, I regard the best explanation to reside in the fact that Jos 8:30-35 comprises both an ideological and a literary typology of structure. As we have seen, the Ark of the Covenant was a recurring factor in the preceding sections: the crossing of the Jordan, the circuits around Jericho, the ritual lamentation after the defeat at Ai, and now, also, on Mt. Ebal. It appears that the Deuteronomist has here made use of older materials to weave a composition and textual structure ultimately dependent on the relation between Moses and Joshua. In the Book of Joshua the latter is invariably characterized as the one who always does as Moses had commanded. The Deuteronomist's composition is distinguished by an extraordinary emphasis on observance of the Law.[11]

Deut 11 and 27 surely derive from a ceremony whose *Sitz im Leben* is now obscure, but which in the nature of things will have been connected with Shechem. This ceremony, the inscription of the Law on stones and the construction of the altar on Mt. Ebal, is to be performed *when the Israelites have crossed over the Jordan*, according to Deut 27:4. But if this ceremony is to have any content, then a curse must have struck Israel on some occasion. However, this only occurs once in the course of Joshua's conquest, namely when Achan had stolen from the booty that was consecrated to destruction (*ḥērem*) in Jos 7:1ff. Achan is the first Israelite to sin on Canaanite soil[12], and his crime is characterized as breach of covenant in 7:15 (cf. also v. 11 for the collective aspect). This leads to Israel's failure to conquer Ai; Israel is struck down by the curse. Only when Achan has been discovered and expunged from Israel together with his house may Joshua recommence the struggle with Ai (8:1ff), this time victoriously: Israel is again under the blessing. In my opinion the defeat and victory at Ai make up the "textbook example" of curse and blessing, respectively[13]. Thus the occasion arises when the ceremony on Mt. Ebal is appropriate; however, it is inconceivable that the Deuteronomist intends to describe an actual or historical event here, since his intentions are ideological. He is following the notice in Deut 11:30, where both Garizim and Ebal are described as situated *mūl haggilgāl*. It is very difficult to say just where *this* geographical datum originated, though the author may have been the Deuteronomist; if so, he will have intended his original reference to Ebal to bring Jos 8:30-35 within the geographical context represented by Jos 1:1-8:29, and within the ideological context provided by the unsuccessful and successful campaigns against Ai. Thus the presence of the Ark of the Covenant on "Ebal" in 8:33 would be unremarkable (cf. Zobel 1973, col. 403; see also 7:6). Like the Ark, the people are based on Gilgal, as we learn from the treaty with the Gibeonites in Jos 9:6.

Victory – Defeat – Victory – Altar Construction:

The theme of blessing and cursing is extremely common in Deuteronomistic historical writing, but its occurrence in Jos 7-8 is nevertheless quite striking, since it is the only occasion on which Joshua is connected with a defeat caused by a breach of covenant. As I have attempted to illustrate, one of the Deuteronomist's guiding principles in the composition of the Book of Joshua is to show that Joshua's behaviour corresponds to that of Moses. Joshua had already received the instruction to build an altar on Mt. Ebal in Deut 27, and the chronological stipulation "on the day you pass over the Jordan" was expressly emphasized. The location of the altar passage Jos 8:30ff. can now be literarily explained, since the segment composed of Jos 3-8 has the same structure and design as Exod 12-17.

After the spectacular victory over the Egyptians, Exod 15:22ff. describes the people's apostasy in a series of episodes culminating in their accusation against Yahweh at the waters of Massah and Meribah (Exod 17:1-7). The succeeding verses relate how Amalek seeks to overcome Israel; just as at the Sea of Reeds, victory is won when Moses raises his "rod of God", while Joshua leads the actual fighting. But the event itself is scarcely spectacular; Moses is unable to hold his hands aloft until Amalek is defeated. The reason for this is probably to be seen in the people's contention with Yahweh: the "waters of Meribah" became the definitive reason why Moses had to die east of the Jordan in Num 27:14, while in Deut 6:16; 9:22; 33:8 the episode is described as an unambiguous breach of covenant. Comparison of the events at Rephidim (Exod 17:8-16) with those at Ai (Jos 7-8) is indeed rather striking. Joshua extends his *kīdōn* (Jos 8:18), since the "rod of God" is reserved for Moses alone. But it is interesting to observe that directly after the battle at Rephidim Moses constructs an altar (Exod 17:15) so that the event is written down and inculcated into Joshua. Thus, in order to emulate Moses, Joshua too constructs an altar after the victory at Ai. This requires the ideological and literarily typological conceptions of the Deuteronomist. The geographical context is of scant significance; Joshua had to build an altar, and the one on Mt. Ebal was the only one he was commissioned to build (in Deut 27:5).

It will now be appropriate to juxtapose the textual structures we have compared here (Malamat 1979):

Exod 12-17   *Jos 3-8*

Ch. 12-14 celebration of Passover   Ch. 3-6 crossing of the Jordan
       crossing the Sea of Reeds   celebration of Passover
       destruction of the Egypt-   Jericho consecrated to
       ians, Exod 14:28   destruction

Ch. 15-17	Waters of Marah, Elim	Ch. 7-8	defeat at Ai
(apos-	and esp. Massah-Meribah		breach of covenant
tasy)	defeat and victory at		
	Rephidim		
	Moses' "rod of God" (hands)		Joshua's *kīdōn*
	construction of altar		altar on Mt.Ebal

II. The Deuteronomistic Conceptions of the Land in the Book of Joshua

From a geographical point of view, the Book of Joshua is a veritable gold mine. There are practically no placenames in the rest of the Old Testament which are not mentioned in Joshua (North 1979, pp. 36ff). Such a compilation of names implies a "history" which covers an appreciable timespan. With some exceptions, the tribal boundaries may well go back to pre-Davidic times. Concerning the stereotypical formal language which is used in connexion with boundary lists, it will no doubt have been a simple matter to append name after name. This way of reproducing geography need not have any directly ideological background, if one here excepts the statistically disproportionate occurrence of names connected to the territory of Judah. Generally speaking, it is the case that the farther the tradent's description leads us from Jerusalem, the more diffuse are his impressions as to the contours of his map.

However, there is one context in which the tradent is quite sure of his geography: this is where he assigns to various areas borderlines that have ideological implications. In addition to utilizing traditional tribal borders, the Deuteronomist operates with a number of conceptions of the land. The situation of the divided kingdom appears within the sections dealing with the Conquest and the assignment of territory by lot. It is the borders of Greater Judah, that is, the Southern Kingdom, which dominates the section dealing with the Conquest (cf. Kallai 1960 and 1978). From Jericho, Ai, and Gibeon Joshua follows the northern boundary of the kingdom of Judah, and, according to Jos 10:41, its southern boundary extends "from Kadesh-barnea to Gaza, and all the country of Goshen, as far as Gibeon". We shall shortly observe how ideologically exactly the northern border of Judah is delineated in the Book of Joshua.

The Divided Monarchy, however, does not represent any idealized situation; rather, this role is assigned to the United Monarchy, the Kingdom of David. Its north-western border is described during Joshua's pursuit of his enemies after the battle at the waters of Merom. The Israelite forces are said to stop at Great Sidon and Misrephoth Ma'im in Jos 11:8 (cf. Jos 13:6). In reality, the Deuteronomist uses this sort of geographical notice to delineate the actual kingdom of David. In my opinion the Deuteronomist seeks in the Book of Joshua precisely to describe the extent of this kingdom; in short, the tradent has taken his point of departure in the allotment traditions stemming from Shiloh and composed his description of the Conquest so that it accords with the allotment scheme. The Deuteronomistic sections of text emphasize the incorporation of the regions east of the Jordan into this area. The concept of "Canaan" plays a subordinate role in the Book of Joshua. Admittedly, certain events do occur on the western side of the Jordan, so that one should have some reason to enquire as to location, but it should be observed that the term "Canaan" properly appears in Jos 14:1, which introduces Joshua's allotment of Cis-Jordan, cf. 5:12. The expression which is otherwise associated with the land of Canaan is "the land which Yahweh swore to give to their fathers"; this occurs four times, in Jos 1:6; 5:6; 21:43. 44. Jos 1:6 implies that Joshua will allot the land, and in 5:6 we read the well-known designation, "a land flowing with milk and honey". The expression "all the land which he swore to give to their fathers" recurs in the Deuteronomistic summary in Jos 21:43f; this clearly refers to Canaan (cf. Jos 22:4). But in the Book of Joshua Canaan only comprises part of the Deuteronomistic conception of the land, since the eastern tribes of Gad and Reuben, plus the half-tribe of Manasseh also belong to the Israelite totality. Thus Joshua's first orders in ch. 1:2 are addressed to these eastern tribes, to whom Moses had given land (Num 32; Deut 2:24ff). Moreover, the eastern tribes regularly reappear as necessary components of the Deuteronomistic view of the land; see Jos 12:1-6; 13:7ff.; 20:8; 21:36ff.; 22:1ff. By means of a simple geographical scheme based on the four points of the compass the area is represented which comprised the historical extent of the Davidic empire as it is depicted in 2 Sam 24. Jos 22 describes the east-west axis, while Jos 24 accounts for the north-south axis.

However, these features do not completely exhaust the conceptions of the land entertained by the Deuteronomist, since even greater

perspectives are also offered. The description of the land which introduces the Book of Joshua in 1:4 makes up a gigantic area between the
Euphrates and the Mediterranean, the Lebanon and the desert. It is an
original piece, since the people are here gathered east of the Jordan
and Joshua does not allot any more land than is in fact contained by
Cis-Jordan. In other words, this geographical significance: the Israelites
neither conquer nor apportion this colossal area (cf. 1 Chron 5).

A sort of reservation is adumbrated in 1:3, where the Israelites
are told that "Every place that the sole of your foot will tread upon I
have given to you, as I promised to Moses." This presumably refers to
the territories which Israel was capable of conquering. The expression
is also to be found in Deut 11:24 in conjunction with the same
description of the land as at Jos 1 and Jos 14:9, which refer to Caleb
and his inheritance.

Interestingly, a similar territory is described in Ps 80 in the language
of metaphor. The psalm seems to be of North Israelite provenance, as
it contains such names as Joseph, Ephraim, Benjamin, and Manasseh.
Another peculiarity is that "Sebaoth" seems to be used as a proper
name. From v. 9 (Eng. 8) the text reads,

> Thou didst bring a vine out of Egypt,
> thou didst drive out the nations and plant it.
> Thou didst clear the ground for it;
> it took deep root and filled the land.
> The mountains were covered with its shade,
> and El's cedars with its branches;
> it sent out its branches to the sea,
> and its shoots to the River[14].

It will be noted that the same territory that is mentioned in Jos 1:4
is here connected with the Exodus from Egypt; it is otherwise associated with the idealized extent of the Davidic kingdom in Zech 9.

The description of the region in question occurs in at least one context which will no doubt have been of great importance to the Deuteronomist, namely that of the making of law and obedience to it. Thus
Exod 23:31 represents the same land which (it is hoped) will become
Israel's possession, while at the same time giving directives for the
people's existence in the land. Deut 1:1-8 also summarizes this enormous area in the context of Moses's exposition of the Law for the
people. Further, Jos 1:4 is situated in a context in which Joshua is

enjoined to adhere to the Law by reciting it both day and night. The phrase of reassurance, the injunction to "be strong and of good courage" recurs time and time again in the first chapter of the Book of Joshua; note the same terminology in Ps 80:16ff, where it is addressed to "the king". This connexion between land and legal observance is even more apparent in Deut 11:22ff:

> For if you will be careful to do all this commandment which I command you to do, loving Yahweh your God, walking in all his ways, and cleaving to him, then Yahweh will drive out all these nations before you, and you will dispossess nations greater and mightier than yourselves. Every place on which the sole of your foot treads shall be from the wilderness and Lebanon and from the River, the river Euphrates, to the western sea."

It could not be more clearly expressed that observance of the Law has been systematically stipulated as the precondition for achieving such a large territory. This area is identical with world rulership, that is, it is the area to which Yahweh lays claim and from which he will direct the course of history. There are numerous examples of this theme in the Old Testament, not the least of them being the classical passage at Amos 9:7[15]. However, mastery of such an enormous territory is held to be contingent upon complete observance of the laws (Deut 11:22ff), but, as this never occurred, the condition persisted as a dreamlike idealization (cf. 1 Kgs 5:1). The origin of this territorial description is surely to be seen in Gen 2:10-14, where the region described by the rivers is interpreted as "Paradise". This habitation is also associated with legal observance in Gen 3:17, and when man's relation to God is sundered, man is expelled and relocated "east of Eden" (Gen 4:16), that is, east of the Euphrates. However, the election of Abraham (Gen 12:1ff) makes possible the recrossing of the Euphrates and the return to "the old territory" by his "heirs". Thus the Primeval History adds a number of typological conceptions to the historical sequence of events surrounding Israel and the land (I am thinking of the removal into exile and the subsequent return).

Already in the Book of Joshua we note signs of incipient apostasy in spite of the activity of an ideal leader such as Joshua. For example, the Israelites make a covenant with Rahab, the first Canaanite they encounter, in spite of explicit legal injunctions to the contrary (Exod 23:32, etc.). The Deuteronomist accordingly does everything in his power to "housebreak" her (Jos 2:9-11). Nevertheless, we subsequently read of Achan's breach of the *ḥērem* regulations, and of Israelite laxity in the matter of the Gibeonites' stratagem. According to the Deuteronomistic scheme of things, the edges of the great idealized kingdom are chipped away by each successive infraction. But Israel's sins continue to multiply without cease, so that after Manasseh there is no longer any warrant for ownership of the land; not even Judah and Jerusalem are conceded any right to continued existence in 2 Kgs 23:26f.

There is one further passage which we only referred to *en passant* above, namely Gen 15:18; it is here the idealized conception of the land occurs for the first time. In my opinion, it is in the present form of the Abraham traditions that we are to seek the background for the composition of the Book of Joshua. As we have seen, Joshua begins with the "Landtag" at Shechem, Jos 24 (but cf. LXX, which replaces Shechem with Shiloh). It was in Shechem that the promise of the land was first pronounced, in Gen 12:7. Quite simply put, between Gen 12:7 and 15:18 we find the conceptions of the land which subsequently appear in the Book of Joshua. In Gen 13 Abraham and Lot are in exactly the same place as the troops detailed for Joshua's ambush in Jos 8, that is, between Bethel and Ai, on the border between the Northern and Southern Kingdoms[16]. Abraham is accorded Cis-Jordan, while Lot receives Trans-Jordan. Abraham later conquers Trans-Jordan in Gen 14; he also pursues his enemies up to Dan, which was the ideological border of the Davidic kingdom, and in Gen 15:18 we hear of a promise concerning the entirety of the ideal territory between the Brook of Egypt and the Euphrates. The area described in Gen 13 and 14 is precisely the region which is subjugated and apportioned out in the Book of Joshua, and which is in principle identical with the empire of David. No matter what historical background underlies Jos 24, the speeches of Joshua now comprise the Deuteronomist's textbook example of how, according to him, Rehoboam should have comported himself in Shechem (1 Kgs 12) in order to retain the integrity of the Davidic empire. The phrase "other gods" is repeatedly used in Jos 24 as a warning to Israel, while in 1 Kgs 12 the apostasy has taken place. Solomon's harem has led the King to serve "other gods", and this entails the first disintegration, the division into north and south. This division is presupposed in the Book of Joshua, and compositionally considered Jos 24 and 22 are show-piece chapters which bring about the reunification of the Davidic empire at all points of the compass. If the

composition at Gen 12:1ff. is the work of a P tradent conceived along
the lines envisioned by Engnell, then the Deuteronomist appears to
have utilised this tradent's composition to form the ideologically laden
document known as the Book of Joshua. Moreover, the latter comprises a programme according to which the entire subsequent historical
development from Judges to the Books of Kings is condemned.

III. Historical Information in the Book of Joshua

The Deuteronomist's way of working with textual structures of the sort
presupposed in these pages demands with all desirable clarity a negative evaluation of the "Conquest" understood as a tangible historical
event datable to 1200 or even earlier[17]. We have instead to do with a
Deuteronomistic authorship which made use of older traditional materials which were no doubt orally preserved and collected at local sanctuaries or cult centres. In this fashion the Deuteronomist created a written programme with an ideal leader of a unified Israel.

The dominant theme in the Book of Joshua is geographical; indeed,
it is a question of "telescoped geography". Starting with the conquest
of the Southern Kingdom (Greater Judah) in Jos 2-10, the land is "re-
captured" up to the extent of the Davidic borders. Here "geography
maskerades as history". The Deuteronomist's way of writing history reveals no attempt at objectivity in any modern sense. However, if we
compare some of his references with extra-Biblical materials we may
not only discover the age of the traditions utilized by the Deuteronomist, but in certain cases we are able to detect tensions between his
adopted materials[18] and his own Tendenz.

The historical question about the fall of Jericho (Jos 6) will doubtless never be resolved, owing to the state of the archeological evidence.
On the other hand, the *ḥērem* regulations which Jos 6 reveals offer a
possible chronological background. As noted previously, they are unimaginably rigorous: all life is to be eradicated, and all booty is accorded to Yahweh (Jos 6:17). It is this stringency that leads to the
harsh judgement on Achan.

In contrast, the Deuteronomistic understanding of *ḥērem* is somewhat more lenient; although here, too, human life is expected to be
wiped out (8:24f; cf. 6:21), the Deuteronomists permit the taking of

booty of both goods and livestock (8:2). The catalogue of plunder in Jos 24:13 includes towns, vineyards, and olive groves. The Deuteronomistic view which permits the taking of life while admitting the right to plunder is naturally realistic; this is indicated by comparison with the lists of booty published by the Assyrian kings (cf. Elat 1977, pp. 209ff).

Furthermore, the destruction is invariably signalled by an oracle. In Jos 6:2 Yahweh announces to Joshua, "See, I have given into your hand Jericho, with its king and mighty men of valour", and in 8:1, "take all the fighting men with you, and arise, go up to Ai; see, I have given into your hand the king of Ai, and his people, his city, and his land". Similar formulaic language is to be found in the Moabite Stele, line 14: "And Chemosh said to me, 'go, take Nebo'". From the continuation of this it emerges that, as practised by the Moabites, *ḥērem* was identical to the procedure described in Jos 6. In lines 11-18 king Mesha remarks that,

> I fought against the town (against Ataroth), and I took it and slew all the people of the city as a (*riyyat* or *rawyat*) sacrifice to Chemosh and Moab, and from there I brought back the altar-hearth of his Dod and brought it before Chemosh in Keriyoth . . . Go, take Nebo from Israel. So I went by night and fought against it from dawn to midday, and I took it and killed all of them, 7,000 men, men, women, and slaves, because I had consecrated it to destruction to Ashtar-Chemosh. And I took from there Yahweh's cultic implements and brought them before Chemosh (see e.g. van Zyl 1960, pp 190f).

What the "implements" in question may have been cannot be discovered on the basis of the text, but it will probably not be too daring to compare them with the metals mentioned in Jos 6. The Moabite Stele says nothing about other types of booty.

The correspondence between the *ḥērem* principle in the Moabite Stele with that in Jos 6 and the latter chapter's non-Deuteronomistic origin suggests an approximate date for the relaxation of the stringency of the principle. The antiquity of the principle as well as its association with Gilgal/Jericho is confirmed via yet another Old Testament text namely 1 Sam 15. Saul is here ordered (in 15:3) to "go and smite Amalek, and utterly destroy all that they have; do not spare them, but kill both man and woman, infant, suckling, ox and sheep, camel and ass (cf. Jos 6:21)." However, Saul breaks with the radical *ḥērem* principle

and is accordingly condemned by Samuel in Gilgal. Thus it would be
logical to suppose that Jos 6 belonged to the Gilgal materials, like Jos
7, where Achan's treachery is virtually identical to Saul's in 1 Sam 15.
In this connexion it is by no means inconceivable that *wayyissob* in
1 Sam 15:12 implies that the Ark of the Covenant was Saul's personal
property (cf. Jos 6 and 7), and that it was attached to Gilgal.

It is possible to use the evidence of the Moabite Stele as we have
done in connexion with the concept of *ḥērem* in two other cases, and
thereby to indicate some chronological relation to the Deuteronomist.
In line 10 the Moabite Stele reads "and the men of Gad had dwelt
in the land of Ataroth from of old (*mē'ōlām*)." The city of Ataroth is
supposed to have been located about 18 km northwest of Dibon (Ottosson 1969, pp. 80f). The only text in the Old Testament which mentions the Gadites as dwelling in the vicinity of Ataroth is Num 32,
which is assuredly a P text. No other alternative is possible, since in
the Book of Joshua the Deuteronomist consistently locates the tribe of
Reuben in the area the Moabite Stele and Num 32 assign to Gad (Jos
13:15ff). Thus the Deuteronomist concentrates on the genealogical
history, while P is well informed as to actual dwelling-conditions
to the east of the Jordan, at least in the period around 850 BC.

Somewhat more conjecturally, it is possible that the Moabite Stele
can provide some background to the situation in Jos 22, which deals
with the construction of an altar by the east Jordanian tribes. Unquestionably, the chapter relies on P traditions, as a brief comparison
with (not least) Num 32 shows. Already in Jos 22:10f. the location of
this altar is unclear, and there has been no lack of exegetical suggestions. Here line 12 of the Moabite Stele, which mentions "Dod's al-
tar-hearth in Ataroth", may offer a viable clue. The Reubenites and
Gadites (the order is that of the Deuteronomist) figure as the main ac-
tors in Jos 22, which suggests that the chapter may be able to shed light
on conditions in southern Trans-Jordan. The Moabite Stele indicates
that the Israelite cult was observed in Gadite territory. It may be pure
coincidence, but is nevertheless worth noting, that the name *'ar'ēlī*
(cf. the *'r'l* of the Moabite Stele) is also found among those Gadites
who went down to Egypt in Gen 46:16 and returned from Egypt in
Num 26:17. Jos 22:22ff. contains covenantal formulas (cf. Boecker
1964 pp. 31ff; Snaith 1978), and it is in reference to these that the altar becomes a witness to the commonalty between east and west. It

is important to the Deuteronomist that the altar be sanctioned; otherwise the contiguity of the Davidic empire would have been jeopardized.

In 1967 a significant textual find was made at *tell dēr 'allā*, which is situated to the east of the river Jordan immediately north of *wādī ez-zerkā*. The text, known as the *dēr 'allā* inscription, consists of fragments of text written in black and red ink on plaster. It is dated archeologically to 400 BC (Franken 1967), but paleographically to the eighth century (Naveh, 1967). Opinions on this text are divided on many issues[19], but at least one matter is abundantly clear: that the protagonist in the inscription is "Balaam, the son of Beor, the man who was the seer of the gods". This find has naturally served to set the narratives about Balaam ben Beor in the Old Testament in relief. There can be no doubt that we have to do with the same Balaam, who thus figures in both cases. The description of Balaam's residence in Num 22:5, *^{a}šer 'al-hannāhār 'eres b^{e}nē-'ammō*, has been regarded as obscure, but the find at *dēr 'allā*, which will most likely have been Balaam's home region, suggests that the reading *b^{e}nē-'ammōn* is correct[20]. The Jabbok, the modern *wādī zerkā*, is always seen in the Old Testament as the river boundary of the Ammonite territory (Simons 1947, pp. 96f.). In short, that this was the geographical location of Balaam's home may now be regarded as assured. However, there are chronological complications. Balaam is associated in the Old Testament with the Mosaic era, which we generally date to about 1200 BC. The Deuteronomist knows Balaam and associates him with the five Midianite kings and with the Amorite king Sihon in Jos 13:21, a passage that must be dependent upon the information provided by Num 31:8. Now, although the dating of the *dēr 'allā* inscription must be regarded as uncertain, there is much to suggest that it is to be included among the same Trans-Jordanian materials as the Moabite Stele. As we have observed, the information in these materials must be taken into consideration in any attempt to evaluate the understanding of history promulgated by the P passages in question. In the same fashion, a re-evaluation of the chronology of the OT Balaam narrative is required by the *dēr 'allā* inscription, but here it is interesting to note that it is P who has preserved the traditions in question.

Yet another archeological text find helps to illuminate the relationship between P and the Deuteronomist; the find in question is comprised of the Ostraca of Samaria (Reisner 1924, pp. 229f). These ostraca are dated to the period shortly before the fall of the Northern Kingdom (Yadin 1961). Among the names which feature on the ostraca, the following are of considerable interest: Abiezer (2 x), Helek (6 x), Shechem (2 x), Shemida (14 x), Noah (1 x), and Hoglah (4 x). The first four names correspond to some of the names of the sons of Gilead which are mentioned in Num 26:30-32. According to Num 26:33; 27:1ff, and 36:11 Noah and Hoglah are among the names of the daughters of Zelophehad. In other words, every one of the names listed here is demonstrably rooted in North Israelite history. They crop up in a formulaic context, supplied with the prefix l^e, and thus designate either the receivers or the owners of the wine or oil jars in which the inscriptions were incised. Although all of these ostraca have been excavated in Samaria, it is by no means obvious that the names must be associated with this locality. According to the P traditions preserved in Num 26:29ff, the names of the sons of Gilead and Zelophehad's daughters are not assigned to any part of the tribe of Manasseh; rather, the name of Gilead is geographically linked with Trans-Jordan. But in Jos 17:1 the Deuteronomist has shattered the genealogy of Manasseh in such a way that he has reassigned both the sons of Gilead and Zelophehad's daughters (the sixth generation) to "the rest of the tribe of Manasseh" in *Cis-Jordan*.

In Jos 17:6 the land of Gilead falls to "the rest of the Manassites", although the remark is not further explained. The Deuteronomist's relocation to Cis-Jordan of the Manassites mentioned above is thus substantiated by the Samaria Ostraca. Now, the river Jordan will scarcely have been an impassible boundary river separating the two parts of the tribe of Manasseh during the hegemony of the Northern Kingdom. The division of the Manassites in this manner is typical of the Deuteronomist; compare, for example, the expression "half of the sons of Machir" in Jos 13:31. The origin of the Deuteronomist's "historiography" will in this instance surely have been that Machir had resided in Cis-Jordan from the beginning (Ottosson 1969, pp. 138ff). In fact, it is plausible that Jos 17:18 refers to Trans-Jordan (Noth 1953, ad loc.). It is undeniable that the Deuteronomist had at his disposal historical information which was quite detailed; but we should again note that here, too, his information concerns condi-

tions at a rather late time, in this case around 740 BC. The Deuteronomist affords us a limited but interesting insight into the administ-
ration of the Northern Kingdom; P, on the other hand, was scarcely
concerned with such matters.

The settlement of the region to the west of the river Jordan is
otherwise related in the texts describing the allotment of the land;
these are linked with Shiloh in Jos 14:1, and we must suppose that
they were preserved by the priesthood of the Shiloh sanctuary. Apart
from the north-south constellation of the Deuteronomist (Jos 14-17),
that is, the Divided Kingdom, it is entirely conceivable that the division of tribes harks back to the borders of Saul's kingdom (2 Sam
2:9). In support of this, we should note that according to the Deuteronomist, Judah too, like Ephraim and Manasseh, receives its allotment in Gilgal, while that of Benjamin is determined in Shiloh (Jos
18:11). These conditions could possibly reflect the Saulid era. At the
allotment Benjamin belongs to the northern group of tribes, even
though the Deuteronomist's war of conquest takes place on Benja-
minite   territory. In any case, since the Amarna period the northern
border of Benjamin formed a natural division between north and
south[21], and it is also ideologically laden by virtue of the fact that
Abraham pitches his tent and builds an altar between Bethel and Ai;
see Gen 12:8; Jos 7:2; 8:9. In the Book of Joshua the Deuteronomist has constructed an ideological and programmatic version of history and attempted to assimilate into it the apportionment details from
the Shiloh sanctuary. Topographically speaking, Benjamin's territory
belongs together with that of Judah.

Engnell's description of P as a responsible tradent and publisher of
the "P Work", or Tetrateuch, whose most notable feature is a stylistic formalism of considerable antiquity, and which generically
is the sort of material pertaining to the office of a royal antiquary, is
still relevant today. The southern orientation of the "P Work" must,
however, be admitted, though there is also "northern" P material[22]. P
will quite naturally have been represented at all cult centres, no matter where situated in the country. Engnell would surely never have
admitted that P plays the role in the Book of Joshua which I have
attempted to demonstrate here.

After having conducted an in-depth study of the Book of Joshua,
and having performed an analysis of the language and style of P, while

keeping a weather eye on the Tetrateuch[23], my characterization of P is as follows:

P was a widespread phenomenon attached to priestly circles at the regional sanctuaries in Palestine. A characteristic priestly language was generated by a milieu embracing liturgies, recitations, laws, and so forth. The tradition was of impressive antiquity, but it continued to be transmitted as long as the Temple functioned. In other words, we have no indications of a specially delimited, post-Exilic P source, and if it existed at all it will have represented the final stage of the process of tradition. In other words, P was a process whose material had acquired its special characteristics at an early date. We discover the language of P in the Book of Joshua when the Deuteronomist makes use of salvation history and of historical materials which must have been employed and preserved in the Temple. The priests and related circles will have functioned as collectors of such legends and traditions as the Rahab narrative, the story of the Gibeonites' stratagem, the defeat at Ai, the fall of Jericho, the altar on the other side of the Jordan, and so forth. The allotment materials, which seem to reflect the period of Saul, will have been attached to Shiloh.

As a geographer, the Deuteronomist has an ideological bias, but in spite of the fact that this Tendenz gives his work a schematic character it is nevertheless reliable. The geography of the Book of Joshua is almost unimaginably compressed, and it is evident that its materials cover a broad chronological spectrum. As an historian, the Deuteronomist often encounters serious problems, owing to the fact that reality does not develop in ideological sequences. Thus, in particular, the Deuteronomist's depiction of the Conquest is to be followed with considerable caution, as it has been both compressed and more or less created by the Deuteronomist. The ideological aversion of the Deuteronomist and Jerusalem to all that North Israel stands for is based on historical realities which had been tangible since the Amarna period. But the notion of an hegemony of the Southern over the Northern Kingdom, thus forming a unified monarchy, which is promulgated by the Deuteronomist, has no basis in historical tradition[24]. To the contrary, history reveals that the Northern Kingdom's attempts to dominate the Southern Kingdom was a tradition persisting from Lab'ayu in the Amarna period to Saul, Ishba'al, and later figures.

SELECTED ASPECTS OF NORDIC TRADITIO–HISTORICAL PSALM RESEARCH SINCE ENGNELL: LIMITATIONS AND POSSIBILITIES

Anders Jørgen Bjørndalen

In the last decades of the life and work of Sigmund Mowinckel,[1] who among other things was a remarkable interpreter of the psalms, Ivan Engnell appeared in Sweden with a programme for studying the Old Testament that was in large measure his own creation (Engnell 1943, pp. 174-177)[2]. However, this programme does reveal that Engnell had received strong impulses from others[3], not least of these being Mowinckel's consistently elaborated view of the Old Testament Psalms as pre-exilic cultic poetry which had grown out of, was formed by, and utilized in, the cult (cf. Mowinckel 1921, pp. 134ff and 1922, pp. 16ff *et passim*)[4]. Nevertheless, as suggested above, Engnell's research programme was an independent development which came to exercise a tangible influence[5] on the direction which Engnell had termed traditio-historical research.

Against this background it would be appropriate to examine Engnell's traditio-historical programme in connexion with psalm research, if we are to attempt to point to the various tendencies in recent traditio-historical study of the psalms here in the Nordic countries. This is especially appropriate inasmuch as Engnell applied his traditio-historical concept to the psalms differently than he did to other Old Testament materials.

Engnell's programme for studying the psalms has been reviewed from several vantage points by Svend Holm-Nielsen (1955, pp. 137ff. 203, n. 131) and Arvid S. Kapelrud (1965, pp. 81-86 and 1966, pp. 87ff), but not to any significant extent by Douglas A. Knight (1973, pp. 267. 268). I shall confine myself here to mentioning a few basic characteristics.

Engnell's approach to the psalms is adumbrated, as far as the royal ideological elements are concerned, in his doctoral dissertation (1943, pp. 176f), and concerning "form literary" views on the Old Testament in his traditio-historical introduction (1945, pp. 52ff.). In both works Engnell strongly emphasized a thoroughly cultic under-

107

standing of the psalms. Furthermore, he describes his programme fairly thoroughly in his article "Psaltaren" in *SBU* II, here largely cited
after the second edition (1962-63 II, cols. 618-57).

To begin with there is nothing very striking about Engnell's traditio-historical series of questions for psalm study, except that all of
them are termed traditio-historical. The series will doubtless be well
known:

> the question of oral or (1962-63 II, col. 1256) written tradition
> and fixation;
> literary form, and the like;
> Sitz im Leben of the psalms and the Psalter;
> their process of creation and
> their use, etc.

The *tools* mentioned by Engnell are correspondingly comprehensive: all available criteria and means of assistance may be employed,
even those which refer to contents, as well as linguistic, idea-historical,
comparative criteria, and so forth. Looking back on this register of
questions and procedures, Engnell speaks of "such a collected evaluation of a traditio-historical nature . . . " (1962-63 II, col. 621).

Concerning the Sitz im Leben, process of creation, and use of the
psalms Engnell powerfully wields Mowinckel's discovery that the
psalms are *in principle cultic poetry*. The traditio-historical interpretation of them presupposes "as fundamental an in-principle cultic interpretation of the psalms" (col. 621)[6]. Here we find in Engnell's
work a point of departure from which he derives a number of important hypotheses with only minor qualifications[7]. I instance the
following three theses:

> The psalms of the psalter will for the most part have been com-
> posed by priestly and prophetic cultic functionaries at diverse
> sanctuaries in Canaan, and in the last instance at the Temple in
> Jerusalem (col. 621)[8].
> Since they were cultic texts, "(one) should . . . probably be able
> to assume that" the psalms were written down at an early point
> and that these literarily fixed texts will have been preserved as nor-
> mative, ritual, and sacred *Vorlagen* which ensured an unchangeable
> and correct transmission (col. 622)[9].
> "But it is equally certain, if not more so, that the modification and

use of these cultic songs was based upon oral tradition: they will have been 'preserved in the heart', i.e., one learned them by rote and surely memorized them scrupulously, in accordance with the great importance which is always assigned to the in every detail absolutely invariant recitation of central cultic texts in conjunction with the sacral actions whose perfect performance was thought to ensure the perpetuation of the people, and upon which the cosmos itself was held to depend" (col. 622).

Here one might ask as to whether Engnell's assumption of the psalms' early literary fixation and of the normative and supportive function of the written text for an absolutely unvarying recitation is an adequate expression of his intentions. It is conceivable that these remarks have been "sharpened" such that their *implicatum* could be expressed with more reserve, not least because Engnell of course sometimes very strongly asserted the reliability of the oral tradition (1945, pp. 40ff)[10].

However, the following considerations suggest that Engnell's formulations here are not so "sharpened":

1) Their likelihood has been carefully weighed; note "possibly" (see n. 7); one "should probably be able to assume that"; "equally certain, if not more so".

2) parallel concepts and amplifying adjectives occur in strong concentration: "normative, ritual, and sacred *Vorlagen*", "unchangeable and correct transmission", "scrupulously memorized", "great importance", "in every detail absolutely invariant recitation". One gets the impression that Engnell is struggling to ensure that the reader will accept that he means just what he says.

3) These views are expressly presented as being an exceptional characteristic of the psalms in the Old Testament, that is, exceptional in relation to other traditional materials in the Old Testament. It is accordingly not to be expected that these insights should correspond to the theoretically conceivable picture of a "living tradition" (1945, p. 42) which Engnell otherwise paints of other Old Testament traditional materials.

4) In connexion with the points mentioned above it is also significant that Engnell did not express himself more reticently, less

sharply, something he under other circumstances was quite capable of.

In conclusion: there is every reason to suppose that Engnell here (intuitively) communicates with his readers in accordance with H.P. Grice's "cooperative principle", and perhaps with his "maxims of conversation" (1975, pp. 45f. 50). He does not express himself incomprehensibly.

Already here Engnell's deductions based on the presumptive cultic status of the psalms rule out on the theoretical plane any attempt to trace various stages in the growth of the individual psalms, since their textual state and form may have been subjected to changes. In connexion with the rest of the Old Testament literature Engnell otherwise *in practice* regarded this as extremely difficult (1945, p. 30; 1962-63 II, cols. 1256f). It seems that Engnell admitted scant room for the notion of "a certain living reformulation" *of the psalms* "in the course of time" (1945, p. 42) during an oral, cultic transmission prior to the Exile, if one ignores the fact that he assumed that a significant number of them were imported and modified North Israelite psalms[11]. According to Engnell, even if the cultic use of the psalms ceased with the fall of Jerusalem in 587, which made their appropriate (i.e., cultic) understanding difficult, the consonantal tradition will have continued fixed and largely unbroken (1962-63 II, cols. 623f). It thus leads us back to the oldest cultic theologoumena of Judah, and in part of Israel.

For Engnell, the picture these theologoumena paint of the Jerusalem cult tradition consists of relatively few and simple lines. Central, indeed "dead-centre" in the picture is the divine king (col. 643, cf. I, col. 405), the *institution* of sacral kingship is the root and branch of psalmic literature as such, in Egypt, in Mesopotamia, and in Canaan (II, col. 643). A minimum of thirty and perhaps as many as sixty *leʾdāwīd* psalms are royal psalms in the sense that the king is the liturgical subject or goal of these sacral activities (col. 630). Engnell held that as a divine king the king was associated in principle in a special way with the dying and rising vegetation god, in Canaan called Dōd (1943, p. 176; 1962-63 I, col. 424; II, cols. 629f). The king suffers in the cultic drama, dies, and resurrects during the New Year Festival in Jerusalem under the monarchy. Furthermore, as Yahweh's servant he also atoned for the people's sin and yet was victorious, proleptically but effectively (II, col. 653) as Yahweh's representative over the powers of chaos as well as over national enemies (I, col. 767).

Although we might be tempted to find the relationship between Dōd and Yahweh fascinating and problematical, Engnell announces drily that "unfortunately our knowledge of the various sides of the royal cult and the function of the sacral king within it is quite inadequate" (II, col. 630). Engnell could not detect any development or notable change within the Jerusalem cult tradition during the monarchy; sacral kingship will have preserved its central position throughout (I, col. 767). All of the decisive aspects of the mythical scheme of the understanding of God will have been established by and during the offical syncretism David brought about in Jerusalem (I, cols. 765ff). Similarly, the considerable importation of North Israelite psalms into Jerusalem did not signify any change in Jerusalem's cultic tradition, as these imported psalms were transformed instead (II, cols. 626f. 631f).

There is no sign that Engnell's picture of the Jerusalem cult tradition under the monarchy left room for any so-called democratization of the royal psalms. On one hand, as mentioned above, the sacral king retained his cultic position throughout the entire period of the monarchy. On the other hand, the psalmic literature of Israel and the rest of the Near East is preserved in "democratic" form although what this latter quantity means is very unclear (1945, p. 58; 1962-63 II, cols. 743f)[12].

What is striking about Engnell's understanding of the tradition history of the Old Testament psalms is, first, his notion of the *congealed* psalmic language which was transmitted without "living reformulation" under the monarchy, and virtually none later on. Moreover, this conclusion was not derived from study of the texts; it was deduced from a principle: that, being cultic texts, the psalms will have been transmitted by an "in every detail absolutely invariant recitation".

Second, it is noteworthy that the religious temperament which made use of the psalms throughout the period of the monarchy seems to have had a conceptual content which by and large remained unchanged. The sacral king will always have been the centre of the cult and the main content of the psalms. Thus Engnell appears to feel that there was always a concealed democratization present in the use of the psalms.

These facts establish a *limitation*; there is no room for questions as to changes in the wording of the psalm texts during their use in pre-exilic times, that is, apart from the adaptation of imported North Israelite psalms in Jerusalem[13]. Thus there is no possibility of seeking pre-exilic changes in the theological formulations of the psalms, with the intention of locating and registering pre-exilic cult psalms in traditio-historical terms in relation to each other. For example, the universalism which Engnell finds in the psalms is already founded on the ideology of sacral kingship, as typically represented by the claim of Yahweh's anointed to world rule in Ps 2 (II, cols. 646f). Prophetic influence is rejected (col. 646). In short, sacral kingship tends to function as an infinitely flexible principle for description and interpretation.

As is well known, Engnell's view that the Old Testament psalmic tradition was influenced by a common Near Eastern ideology which was bound up with sacral kingship encountered considerable resistance from his colleagues. In this connexion I would mention Aage Bentzen (1945 and 1947), Sigmund Mowinckel (1951, pp. 60, n. 24. 61, n.28. 88, n.164. 147f., n.106 etc.), and Svend Holm-Nielsen (1955, pp. 137-40). Holm-Nielsen criticized, not in every respect convincingly, Engnell's notion that the king's sacral-ideological function and its democratization were simultaneous events. Further, he quite convincingly demonstrated that Engnell's thesis concerning a hypothetical ideology of a royal tree of life in Ps 1 (Engnell 1953) is wholly without foundation. Helmer Ringgren (1957, p. 13) also implied that he had considerable reservations about the hypothesis of the dominant role of the royal ideology. At the same time, however, Engnell received support across the board from Gösta Ahlström (1959) in his monograph on Psalm 89.

I shall now undertake briefly to comment on the more significant Nordic contributions to an understanding of the tradition history of the psalms which appeared in 1949 and later, and against this background I will attempt to point to some common elements (see Veijola's critical examination of Ahlström 1959, above pp.36-41).

Helmer Ringgren's article on oral and written tradition in the Old Testament (1949) examined a problem posed by Engnell which has genuinely traditio-historical implications (1945, pp. 42f.; cf. 1948-52 II, col. 791). However, Ringgren's criterium marks a fundamental break with Engnell's *deduction* of an invariant transmission of cultic psalms which was first published in *SBU* three years later (II, col. 792). Ringgren examined duplicate texts to discover if the state of the respective texts would allow us to determine whether they had been orally transmitted or preserved in written form. In the psalms which he subjected to study in this fashion Ringgren discovered both written (1949, pp. 43-45 on Ps 18/2 Sam 22,11.12.45) and oral (Ps 18/2 Sam 22,7.26.38) variations. He accordingly drew the conclusion that in the course of time there had been both an oral and a written process of transmission of the psalms. The limitations of this approach do not so much reside in the use of duplicate psalms, since these may well be representative, as in the interpretation of individual variants[14].

In 1955 Svend Holm-Nielsen entered the scene with a large article on the Old Testament psalm tradition, which he followed up with a major work (1960b). In these pieces Holm-Nielsen was especially concerned with the question of the post-exilic cult and its psalmody, and he examined the understanding of the psalms, not least the canonical ones, in this period. Holm-Nielsen's work in 1955 primarily attempted a study of traditio-historical development in the post-exilic period, but it also made possible questions about changes and development in the pre-exilic psalm tradition (p. 194 and n. 62)[15]. Holm-Nielsen carefully considered the possibility that some late Judaic psalms may have had a cultic use under the circumstances then prevailing (pp. 146ff). Furthermore, he showed that the Jewish learned tradition presupposes earlier use of the canonical psalms in conjunction with the Temple cult, and an awareness that the psalms were cultic poetry (pp. 202f) At the same time Holm-Nielsen indicated that the psalms were capable of both historical and messianic-eschatological interpretation (pp. 203f) which corresponds to tendencies Holm-Nielsen demonstrated in the use of the psalms in prophetic and historical texts (pp. 193ff). These tendencies may have been pre-exilic (p. 199), and Holm-Nielsen was also able to demonstrate their presence in the superscriptions of canonical psalms (pp. 207ff). He further showed that this transformed understanding may be detected in the texts of some of the canonical psalms, and found thus both redactional additions and post-exilic canonical psalms (pp. 211ff)[16].

Holm-Nielsen's principal distinction between a cultic, historical, or eschatological understanding of the psalms is largely determined by Mowinckel's conception of the cult, but it is nevertheless useful.

There *is* a significant difference between the continual reapplication of a psalm to the actual exerciser of a cultic function or role, or to the expectations accruing to such a figure[17], on the one hand, and the application of the psalm in all cases to one particular person at one particular past or future situation (Holm-Nielsen 1955, pp. 193ff). However, cultic psalms or recitatives may also refer to a specific event in the past without the event's losing its actuality for the present[18], as is true, for example, of Exodus. Further, Holm-Nielsen's idea that future expectation in a cultic psalm looks forward to the year's culmination in the New Year Festival (p. 195), a concept adopted from Mowinckel (1922, pp. 133-135.145.149f.159f.219.315f), derives more from cult theory than from the texts.

Holm-Nielsen again raised the problem of post-exilic canonical psalms in his treatment that appeared in 1960, this time building his case on the use of older literature in New Testament, late Jewish, and Old Testament sources (1960b, pp. 11ff). Thus with exemplary caution he attempted to compose a criterium for recognizing post-exilic psalmody: the unstressed use of an individual word or phrase deriving from older literature (pp. 16-23). Using this criterium and some support from other areas Holm-Nielsen found that a small number of psalms were best understood as post-exilic, i.e. Ps. 119; 111; 112; 145; 37; and perhaps 25; 34 (cf. pp. 24-53). The importance of this work is sure to reside in the method evolved for the discrimination of post-exilic psalms (cf. p. 53).

The possibilities for working along these lines have surely not been exhausted, and indeed Holm-Nielsen has himself written a penetrating study on the use of Old Testament materials in the *Hodayot* (1960a). But otherwise, as far as I am aware, no Scandinavian has continued work in this direction. This could be the result of the fact that the criteria for assigning canonical psalms to the post-exilic period remain somewhat vague and uncertain, as Holm-Nielsen has candidly admitted (1960b, pp. 17-23; 1972, p. 36).

On the other hand, it is apparent that there was considerable Jewish psalmody in the post-exilic period (Holm-Nielsen 1955, pp. 213f; 1972, pp. 36f), and therefore, the possibility must remain open that there are a number of post-exilic psalms in the canonical collection, just as a sizable number of redactional additions must be dated to the post-exilic period (see n. 16 above, and Becker 1966). These considerations have and will continue to have great importance for the study of the tradition history of the psalms.

The possibility of tracing the tradition history of the psalms was first taken seriously when Mowinckel managed to create a consensus on the view that the Old Testament psalms were largely *not* post-exilic, but pre-exilic and cultic. This created enough chronological "room" for pursuing the tradition history of the psalms, but this spectrum was not well exploited, since scholars did not pose the joint questions concerning post-exilic psalms and the understanding of psalms in the late period. It may be said to have been typical of Scandinavian research on the psalms in the 1950's that a psalm was regarded as pre-exilic until the opposite was demonstrated, and such demonstration required formidable energy. As late as 1972 Holm-Nielsen found it necessary to dedicate an entire page of a history-of-research section to arguing for the reasonableness of the supposition that psalms were being composed by the Jews in the post-exilic period (pp. 36f.). Thus as far as this writer is aware, it was entirely Holm-Nielsen's achievement that Nordic scholars, though not Ivan Engnell personally, are prepared to accept the post-exilic span in their work.

A long silence reigned between the works of Holm-Nielsen (1955; 1960b), Ringgren (1957), and Ahlström (1959) on one hand, and more recent Scandinavian studies. In 1975 Simone Springer OSB obtained a licentiate degree in Copenhagen on a thesis about the Autumn Festival and the royal psalms from the viewpoint of reinterpretation (cf. Springer 1979). Stig Norin published an examination of the Exodus traditions in 1977, and Inger Ljung's study of the so-called Ebed-YHWH-psalms appeared in 1978. Engnell's conception played no constructive role in any of these treatments, and indeed both Ljung's formulation of the problem and her conclusions break with some important elements in Engnell's position. Engnell's idea of a "frozen" psalm tradition coupled with his aprioristic pre-exilic dating has not provided fertile soil for developing new and better insights. Arvid S. Kapelrud's article, "Tradition and Worship" (1977), is largely a discussion with Mowinckel, but not with Engnell. It appears that a different and more complicated situation is now present, which is probably also more promising. I shall in the following attempt to describe the more prominent parts of this situation from a traditio-historical point of view.

Simone Springer attempts to demonstrate that certain changes have been undertaken in the textual state of the royal psalms such that the previously existing texts have been subjected to reinterpretation. In the most literal sense of the word, this is a traditio-historical understanding of the growth of the texts of the psalms (pp. 112-148). Springer correlates those elements of the contents of the psalms which are actualized by such changes (p. 149) and compares them with analogous data from Israel's environment (pp. 150-173). In the course of her investigations she also attempts to determine which interests motivated the Israelites so to adopt and transform the psalm texts. I offer here a few examples of Springer's theses concerning such reinterpretive changes.

The problem consists in finding substantive evidence for going behind the existing (consonant) text to reconstruct a hypothetical *Vorlage*. To some extent it seems as if Springer commits herself to arguments which are neither falsifiable nor verifiable[19]. Thus she claims that the expression *yōšēb baššāmayim* in Ps 2:4 has been reinterpreted; the reinterpretation of

> 'the one who thrones in the heavens . . . ' consists in the fact that he laughs and scorns and that this laughter is neither the laughter concerning Baal as he was resurrected from the dead (I AB III, 14-16) nor the laughter of a victorious warrior (Ps 60:10), but that of the sovereignly acting one . . . (Springer 1979, p. 114).

Now if the reinterpretation here lies already in the fact that the one who thrones in the heavens laughs and scorns, as Springer suggests, the present writer would presume that the *Vorlage* of Ps 2:4 will have read *yōšēb baššāmayim 'adōnāi*, i.e., a noun clause with a participial subject. However, it is difficult to imagine this clause, which lacks a parallel element, in this context.

As far as a reinterpretation here resides in the fact that the laughter of the one who thrones in the heavens is not the laughter of kindly El rejoicing that mighty Baal is alive (I AB III, 14-16), this would presuppose the existence of a *Vorlage* of Ps 2:4 with just these characteristics, although this is at present unverifiable.

In Ps 2:6b Springer suggests that the phrase will not originally have mentioned Zion; it could just as easily have been another sanctuary, such as Ugarit, though certainly not in conjunction with v. 6a (pp. 114f.)[20]. Here it seems as if we are invited to accept a *Vorlage without* any sentence nucleus, since v. 6b of course only contains an adverbial prepositional phrase, while the subject, predicate, and direct object are grouped in v. 6a. Alternatively, we might accept a *Vorlage* whose sentence nucleus is not reconstructible. Personally, I should regard such a *Vorlage* as unlikely, as the traditio-historical foundation has not been laid.

It is not easy to say what criteria are to be met if we are to accept the plausibility of an hypothetical *Vorlage*. Such a *Vorlage* must have a reasonably satisfactory text and contain a meaning which is plausible in context, and which at the same time invites our *confidence*. An acknowledged example of a well-founded *Vorlage* is the Canaanite reading of Ps 110:3: "From the womb of the morning I have given birth to you like the dew" (p. 141). A non-Israelite *Vorlage* would also be indicated if the text in question now contains an Israelite-Yahwistic element which for one reason or another appears foreign to its context. Such an indication is in fact present, as has often been noted and is also correctly mentioned by Springer in Ps 2:2b (p. 114), which metrically is superfluous in the strophe 2:1-3.

In his monograph Stig Norin has examined the poetic formulation and transmission of the Exodus materials in the Old Testament psalms. Norin has attempted both to date the psalms in question and to describe the formulation of the Exodus materials in each individual case (1977, pp. 110ff). By far the majority of Norin's psalm dates are well founded, and interesting as well. For one thing, the writer brings in new perspectives in his attempt to construct a chronology, notably in his effort to correlate the psalms with the developmental scheme he presents for the development of the traditions of the Tetrateuch/Pentateuch. In the nature of things one must accept that Norin can only argue for certain degrees of probability, and I shall here admit that I regard his dates for the following psalms as quite uncertain, Ps. 114: early monarchy or the time of Josiah (pp. 127f), Ps 66: pre-exilic (pp. 123f), and Ps 77: exilic times (p. 119).

Furthermore, certain of Norin's hypotheses concerning the Exodus materials may be contested; I fail to see how Ps 18:14-20; 29; 74:12-16; and 89:6-19 refer in any way to the Exodus, as Norin claims[21]. Nevertheless, a series of plausibly dated psalms which clearly refer to the Exodus is left; the series stretches from the seventh century to exilic and post-exilic times, so that Norin is able to paint a convincing picture of a secʹ on of the tradition history of these materials. It is worth noting that no poetical Exodus tradition can be traced back to early monarchical times, since Ps 18,29, and 89 do not refer to the Exodus, and an early date for Ps 114 is doubtful[22]. There is apparently a risk with this sort of traditio-historical work that one tends to re-discover an element of a subject in texts or at times where it does not appear to be attested.

In his article of 1977 Arvid S. Kapelrud has in connexion with the psalms pointed to the most significant element of the historical traditions in them. Also, he has indicated the ways these elements entered into a variety of combinations with elements of mythical origin so that new combinations of motifs arose (1977, pp. 115ff. 119ff) Kapelrud emphasized both the ways the cult and its ramifications formed traditions and the ways traditions influenced the cult (pp. 16ff. 123). The latter point is of great significance: a Canaanite inheritance with its own authority represented a challenge which had to be met, for example, precisely in the cultic acclamation of Israel's Yahweh in his theophany. Thus the combination of only slightly modified Canaanite psalms with specifically Israelite elements was understandably necessary, as, for example, in Ps 29 where "Yahweh" has been entered as the name of the god and (so the Massoretes, and for compelling reasons, also Kapelrud) Kadesh in v. 8 (pp. 116f)[23]. (Mowinckel was scarcely correct to assume that Ps 29 was unlikely to have been originally a Canaanite psalm (1951, p. 614, n. 105); rather, this seems entirely probable).

Analogously in Ps 97, Kapelrud, who has a discriminating "feel" for elements of Canaanite provenance, emphasizes the combination in v. 7 whereby 7b is Canaanite and 7a Israelite (p. 117). Similarly, in Ps 47:3-5 Kapelrud finds that Yahweh's name will have been inserted into a Canaanite pattern (p. 117)[24]. Finally, in Ps 99:6 Kapelrud finds the expression of elements which were consciously selected from the Exodus tradition, and inserted in order to state certain important aspects of Yahweh's being. These were that he was more than the rain and storm god of the theophanies (p. 119), being himself a god of history, who had chosen his own people and placed certain demands on his adherents. In this connexion Kapelrud stresses that the intimate combination of mythological terminology and historical allusions was a permanent and dominant characteristic in Israel and Judah over a long span of time. He further asserts that only one decisive historical event, experienced and interpreted as a theophany, can explain such a combination: the Exodus (p. 119).

Each in his own way, Springer, Norin, and Kapelrud all show how fruitful traditio-historical work with the psalms can be. The tracking down of the growth of the psalm texts and the motives for such development, or the wandering of traditional motifs and their reuse in new contexts and combinations may well be able to enrich our historical understanding of the psalms.

The last investigation I shall deal with here is also fruitful, in part for the understanding it offers of the psalms, but primarily because of the discussion there offered as to how they are to be understood. The work in question is Inger Ljung's *Tradition and Interpretation* (1978; cf. Ottosson 1981b and Culley 1980).

In this work Ljung enters the discussion surrounding the so-called Ebed-Yahweh-psalms, but she takes a direction which is completely new to this discussion. Her point of departure is that investigation of the materials usually grouped under this heading reveals a not inconsiderable quantity of the formulas and formulaic expressions which Robert C. Culley had earlier (1967) found in the Psalter. Thus Ljung adopts Culley's terms "formula" and "formulaic system" as heuristic tools for her study (1978, p. 18).

When Ljung distributes the formulas and formula-like expressions isolated by Culley on the psalms, she isolates a group of twenty-six psalms, individual laments and individual psalms of thanksgiving. Each of these contains five or more occurrences of formulas and formulaic systems. She also finds five psalms of hymnic character and exhibiting formulaic language to some extent (p. 19; cf. p. 20). These psalms of lament and thanksgiving comprise the starting group for Ljung's analysis. Her further procedure may be described as a successive reduction of this group of psalms, sometimes involving supplementation and division by means of an extensive set of criteria.

Ljung's most important criteria are the frequency and distribution of such formulaic language as Culley has isolated, the presence of recurrent compositional patterns, and the correlations between these phenomena. The most important results emerging from this procedure are the discoveries of a group of psalms exhibiting a fixed, and thus conventional, structure or composition, the use of a stable formulaic language within considerable sections of this structure, and the fact that the number of formulas exceeds that in the rest of the psalms in the starting group[25]. Similar discriminations are made within a number of psalms (Ps 6:7-8; 18:2-4; 31:6-7; 116:1-2; 143:1-6); this reveals that some parts are more loosely attached to the compositional pattern and/or display fewer examples of formulaic language (cf. p. 88).

Finally, Ljung tabulates elements of content in her starting group such as themes and motifs which could be thought typical of a conjectural Ebed-Yahweh-Psalm-*Gattung* (pp. 95ff). However, the motifs thus isolated are not confined to texts which conform to the conventional compositional pattern described by Ljung. Thus there can be no question of a *common specific Sitz im Leben* for this compositional pattern. To this observation the writer adds that the psalms and psalmic sections which contain this pattern generally display a formulaic language and content which "indicate a function as formulas with general applicability in situations of distress" (p. 108). Moreover, the subject of these psalms can not be identified.

Against this background Inger Ljung rejects the designation "Ebed-Yahweh-Psalms" and the view that they refer to the cultic function of the sacral king during the New Year Festival (pp. 108.109).

I shall break off my somewhat compressed account of Inger Ljung's admirable work here[26], as an evaluation of her achievement would be appropriate at this point. It will certainly be striking for some readers to note that when Ljung decides to adopt Culley's concepts of "formula" and "formulaic system" she announces in a brief subordinate clause that she leaves aside Culley's emphasis on the oral aspect of the transmission of such formulaic texts (Ljung 1978, p. 18). However, there is no doubt that Ljung's decision in this instance is the *only correct possibility*[27]. But critically speaking, one might remark that Ljung also employs expressions which only appear twice in Culley's examination of the Biblical psalms (Culley Nrs. 73-175). Culley believes that these expressions are formulaic because they appear in such great numbers, but he admits that "a single repetition of a phrase is not very strong evidence for its being a formula, and therefore proposes to distinguish between these and expressions which occur three or more times (1967, p. 32). In my opinion we can scarcely draw conclusions from phrases which only occur twice in the pertinent materials (cf. Watters 1976, p. 15). Thus, since Ljung uncritically makes use of expressions occurring three or more times on the same footing with phrases which are only attested twice, there would seem to be a margin of uncertainty attaching to her conclusions. The number of assuredly formulaic expressions is in some cases considerably smaller than Ljung allows. Nevertheless, I should like to add that this does not necessarily entail that the conclusions she has arrived at are to be evaluated negatively[28].

However, some rearrangements could be considered. The thesis concerning the high concentration of formulaic material is not convincing in the case of Ps 6:2-6 and 18:17-20, if one for the sake of preserving a critical minimum ignores phrases which are only attested twice. On the other hand, it is even more correct than Ljung supposes that Ps 143:1-4 contains little formulaic material in relation to v. 7-10.

But regardless of these considerations, Ljung's criteria for a "high" and "low" number of examples of formulaic language are not completely clear. It seems disputable whether Ps 28:1-7 and 116:3-9 may be said to contain a large number of formulas (Ljung 1978, p. 88). Ps 28:1-7 contains four formulas (or three if we ignore one which occurs only twice in the O.T. psalms), and 116:3-9 contains four. Is this a "high" number when we consider that Ps 143:1-4b. 4c-6 is said to contain a "very few" examples of formulaic language (p. 88) when in fact v. 1-4b displays three, counting formulas which are attested three or more times, and six, if one counts those which are only twice attested?[29]

Yet another source of uncertainty arises from the fact that Ljung seems to register both the number of occurrences of formulaic language *per psalm* as well as those in the psalmic sections which have formulaic character. It would seem to offer somewhat more reliable results if she instead noted the number of occurrences of formulaic language per number of *stichoi* in the individual psalms or in the formulaic part of them.

In spite of the fact that it might be interesting to re-examine Ljung's materials in the light of the reservations expressed above, I doubt after the soundings I have undertaken whether her conclusions would be altered significantly.

The problems Inger Ljung has dealt with will undoubtedly be fruitful for the traditio-historical study of the Psalms. There is considerable justice in her quoting A.B. Lord, "The phrases for the ideas most commonly used become more securely fixed than those for less frequent ideas" (Lord 1960, p. 43, cf. Ljung 1978, pp. 11.88.92). One

ought not to be too sure that tradition is always relatively well en-
dowed with formulas. There is a considerable amount of non-formulaic material in the psalms which has *become* tradition in virtue of the
fact that the psalms were transmitted. However, there is also a striking
correlation between the *poverty* of formulas in sections of the psalms
investigated by Ljung and indications of exilic or post-exilic dating
of these sections or psalms (1978, pp. 110ff; on Ps. 22: pp. 119f).
Furthermore, as far as I can see Inger Ljung has convincingly shown
that the formulaic psalms and psalmic sections she has studied do not
reveal any particular attachment to a royal cult associated with the
New Year Festival.

Inger Ljung's approach could also be applied to other psalms which
she has in fact studied, but which might benefit from closer scrutiny.
Her method might also benefit by being expanded to include a study
of parallel pairs, such as William R. Watters (1976, pp. 132f. 133ff)
has done in the case of Lamentations; the limitation on such a procedure, however, consists in the fact that the Psaltar is a limited
textual corpus containing only a small number of formulas, formulaic
systems, and word pairs.

The most recent Nordic contribution to the traditio-historical
study of the psalms is Timo Veijola's study of Ps 89 (1982). Veijola
proposes the following picture of the development of the text: the oldest part of the psalm is a hymn which includes v. 2-3. 6-19. V. 17-19
are a secondary development. The next phase was the addition of v.
4-5 and 20-46, whose stichometrical structure diverges radically from
that of the hymn, and which contains a number of catchwords which
are peculiar to these particular verses within the framework of the
psalm. Yet other catchwords are common both to these verses and to
the old hymn; therefore the addition is not thought to have been an
originally independent poem. It was probably composed as an addition to the hymn. The final phase involved the addition of v. 47-52,
and have a completely special stichometrical structure (cf. pp. 22-46
on the growth of the text).

The additions are localized and dated to Palestine in the late exilic period between ca. 550 and 539 on the basis of criteria involving
the Israelite language, literature, and (theological) history. This analysis offers a picture of the theological tendencies which surfaced in
the psalm in the course of its development. Veijola holds Ps 89 to
represent a broad stream of late-exilic nationalizing and collectivizing

tendencies (pp. 47-118; cf. 133ff). He further designates it a collective psalm of lament (pp. 119-175) intended for use during public lamentation among the populace remaining in Palestine in late exilic times (pp. 176-210). Veijola rejects the notion that the king is the "singer" of Ps 89, since he regards the singular reading of $^{\prime a}b\bar{a}d\bar{e}k\bar{a}$ in v. 51 as text-critically secondary (pp. 113-117). I should like to draw attention here specifically to two types of criteria employed by T. Veijola. First, (p. 22, n. 2), he has critically adopted the stichometrical analysis of O. Loretz and employed it with great caution and even then in conjunction with other, more traditional criteria (Veijola 1982, pp. 23ff). The correspondence demonstrated by Veijola between some of the stichometrical data and the more traditional insights deserves our attention. Second, Veijola dates the additions composed of v. 4-5. 20-46, and 47-52 on the basis of an hypothesis concerning a number of different Deuteronomists who wrote their respective contributions to the Deuteronomistic Historical Work. Here he concentrates especially on the relation to DtrN, but also to Lamentations, among other things (pp. 75ff). The understanding of the historical development of Deuteronomistic language and theology which is both presupposed and elaborated upon here offers the opportunity of dating – on its specific terms – the appropriate texts very precisely. Veijola does not examine the hymn in v. 2-3. 6-16, which he holds to be the oldest part of Ps 89; nor are his criteria for dating the additions applicable here.

This survey of Nordic traditio-historical research on the psalms has hopefully indicated that there is reason to examine each Old Testament psalm individually to determine whether its text may have arisen over a period of time, whether by oral tradition or written sources. Further, we may assume that the psalms have undergone considerable changes, whether this occurred when a psalm was adapted from the Canaanites, during its transmission in the period of the monarchy, in the Northern or Southern kingdoms, or during exilic or post-exilic times. The various phases of the history of an individual psalm must be detected, dated and further characterized as to text, type and relation to the cult.

Not least difficult in this connexion is the dating of pre-exilic psalms and parts of psalms. We lack a *coordinate system* (or several) of the history of the language and theology of the pre-exilic period;

within such a framework it would be possible to correlate individual psalms, more or less as the isolation of the various redactional layers of the Deuteronomistic Historical Work makes it possible to date texts of the exilic period. Isolated efforts in this direction have been tendered for further testing by S. Norin.

Kapelrud and Veijola have demonstrated how fruitful the quest of the *Sitz im Leben* as the seminal instance can be. It is on the other hand a peculiar characteristic of Scandinavian psalm study since Engnell that the history and tradition of the Jerusalemite cult have not attracted scholars' attention. However, from their respective points of view Holm-Nielsen, Springer, and Norin have also contributed to this problematic area. I suspect that it would be useful for the traditio-historical study of the psalms if we attached more importance to the study of the Jebusite, and subsequently, Israelite cultic tradition of Jerusalem, its leading themes and its presumably impressively gripping history. What *were* its themes? What relations obtained among them? *Was* the cult tradition really, and perhaps from as early as the beginnings of the monarchy virtually a closed, systematically thought-out conception (cf. Steck 1972, pp. 9ff)? What cultic functions did the king exercize, and when did the Davidic monarchy receive its sacral characteristics? Did this happen as early as David (cf. Mettinger 1976)[30].

There might also be reason to leave open the possibility that one or another psalm could be non-cultic; a possibility whose appropriateness should be carefully examined. Gillis Gerleman has provided an impulse in this direction. Taking his starting point in his serious reservations concerning Walter Beyerlin's distinction between institutional and non-institutional pleas (*Rettungsaussagen*) for salvation in psalms dealing with deliverance from enemies (Gerleman 1982, p. 39), and in conjunction with his theory about individual laments and psalms of thanksgiving as featuring *David* as the pattern and comforting *exemplum*, Gerleman finds that "the conception of the cult as the decisive genetic factor (becomes) suspect," (p. 47). In this connexion it should be mentioned that C. Westermann may be *understood* in such a way that his determination of the *Gattungen* of the psalms as "the essentials of that which happens in words from man to God: petition and praise", removes from our view the question of the function and significance of the *cult* for Israelite life[31].

To these suggestions I would merely observe that we are possibly running the risk of thinking too small and too analytically about the cult and its role in ancient Israel and Judah. In a number of different contexts Arvid S. Kapelrud has reminded us of indications of the role of the cult as the basis of life (1972, pp. 189.191.193.197) and as the instance which helped to form traditions (1977, pp. 116ff). Is it not possible that we stand in danger of operating in an uncritically anachronistic manner in insisting on distinctions between secular and cultic? The instructions concerning the cultic prayer in Deut 26:1ff presuppose that the farmer encounters Yahweh as the giver of crops in his daily life. Similarly, the description of the priest's speech to Israel's forces prior to battle in Deut 20:2ff *says* that Yahweh himself also enters the conflict (v. 4). The warrior meets Yahweh in battle, or at least, so it appears. Do we then have a significant distinction between daily life and cult, between agriculture, war, history, and "festival" (cf. Hornung 1966)?

STATUS QUAESTIONIS

by Knud Jeppesen and Benedikt Otzen
in collaboration with Svend Holm-Nielsen

As an Old Testament research discipline, tradition history made its appearance between 1920 and 1960 in two variations: 1) the German approach, which was associated with the names of Noth and von Rad, and which in many respects signified an extension of literary critical method. This approach, however, went a step further than its predecessor, in that it concerned itself to a much higher degree with the questions of the prehistory and composition of the traditional sources. 2) the Scandinavian approach, which understood traditio-historical methodology to be centred on the history of the cult, and which accordingly emphasized the significance of the cultic institutions for the development of tradition prior to written fixation. This approach was seen to apply to, among other things, the Enthronement Festival (Mowinckel), the Passover (Pedersen), and sacral kingship (Engnell). A major group of the Scandinavian scholars emphasized the role of oral tradition in their understanding of the process of tradition prior to written fixation. By the same token, these scholars were prone to be sceptical towards literary critical methodology as an adequate investigative approach to the Old Testament materials.

The lectures delivered during this symposium will no doubt give the impression that this sharp distinction between the German and Scandinavian approaches has become somewhat blurred. Moreover, the group discussions of the various contributions served to confirm that Scandinavian traditio-historical research is in the midst of a process of transformation.

The participants in the symposium were divided into eight groups which convened three times to discuss the issues raised. Naturally, the lectures themselves were the main topic of discussion, but the participants also attempted to point forwards and to indicate new pathways for traditio-historical work. It is obvious that such discussions ranged fairly far afield, so that in this short introduction, which represents the editors' impression of the discussions on the basis of reports delivered by the groups and of Holm-Nielsen's review on the last day of the symposium, it will only be possible to present a mere

sketch of the lively exchange of opinions and the many questions
which were raised. We shall confine ourselves to mentioning those
views which repeatedly appeared in the reports, and which thus seem
to be typical of the more central concerns.

Most Scandinavian scholars have inherited from Engnell the notion
that tradition history is *the* method par excellence. However, the concept itself has often been employed as a sort of abracadabra, and scholars have frequently neglected to define more closely just what they
take tradition history to be. Engnell himself was thoroughly convin-
ced of the correctness of his negative attitude towards literary critical
method, which in his opinion represented a modern European "bookish" conception which simply could not do justice to the special character of archaic literature. Against this method he opposed the importance of the presupposition of a long period of oral tradition
which was supplemented by written tradition at an early date only in
the case of a few forms of literature. This confidence in the perseve-
rance of the oral tradition entailed a corresponding confidence in the
reliability of the Massoretic Text. Engnell was not, however, blind to
the value of form critical and compositional analysis, but religio-
historical motif analysis played a major part in his version of tradition
history.

It was characteristic of the group discussions on the problem of
defining tradition history, that is, of delimiting its essence in relation
to other methods, that the scholars present were generally of the
opinion that the concept of "oral tradition" ought not to be stressed
as much as was earlier the case. After all, we only have the written
record; we can not demonstrate the transition from oral to written
form, and, moreover, it is possible that both forms of transmission ran
parallel to each other and reciprocally influenced each other. Nevertheless, it is still worthwhile to seek to develop criteria for deter-
mining the transition from oral to written transmission. To this end
the results of redaction critical and compositional analysis will no
doubt be invaluable.

Furthermore, it is essential to recognize that the materials will
already have received some sort of structure at the oral level. Form
criticism must take account of this fact, perhaps in such a way that it
will become possible to speak of the tradition history of individual
forms. By the same token, traditio-historical study requires that one
attempt to determine the historical situation and the circumstances

which attended the transition from oral to written transmission. Also, one should attempt to discover the conditions which can have brought about changes in the form of a tradition during the course of transmission, whether such changes will have occurred at the oral or written level.

The latter point signifies that historical, cult-historical, and religio-historical motif analyses may still be admitted into the ambit of tradition criticism. And finally, it is admitted that the classical literary critical approach also retains its validity, at least in respect of certain classes of material, since it attempts to discover unevenness in the texts which may indicate breaks in the tradition.

Thus it was repeatedly acknowledged in the course of the group discussions at Sandbjerg that tradition history is not a limited quantity; rather, it would be more appropriate to describe it as a sort of "umbrella" beneath which the other traditional critical methods may be subordinated. Thus the scholars present were prone to define tradition history rather vaguely, in the sense that the Old Testament literature is predominantly traditional literature, that is, it has received its form in the course of a process of transmission, a process which, whether taking place on the oral or the written level, introduced some changes into the materials. Accordingly, the historian of tradition must make use of all available tools in the effort to trace this process forwards to the point when the tradition in question ultimately became fixed in its final literary form. The effort to disclose the pathways of tradition will entail that one attempt to reveal the historical and religious circumstances which created changes in the tradition. And finally, if it should prove possible, the tradition historian should attempt to characterize the conditions which compelled the written fixation of an oral tradition.

Views of the kind recorded above should make it plain that Scandinavian traditio-historical research has resumed contact with more traditional Old Testament research and with, among other things, the previously mentioned German traditio-historical approach. There nevertheless remains a good deal of scepticism towards the German tendency to attempt to describe the evolutionary pathway of an Old Testament text up to the point when the text in question received its final form. The literary critics have attempted to differentiate between a variety of "sources", in which process they frequently make use of rather exaggerated interpolation theories. Subsequently, an attempt is made to push the process further back in order to examine how these "sources" had developed up to the point at which they were combined to form the final literary product.

Several of the participants in the symposium emphasized an approach in which one analyses the final literary product in terms of composition and redaction, for subsequently to move backwards with the utmost caution. This somewhat altered approach was most clearly expressed in the interest voiced in a number of the discussion groups in studying the relationship between D and P rather than, as was typical of much of the earlier German research, mainly concentrating on J.

The discussions were generally preoccupied with the questions of D and the Deuteronomistic Historical Work. Scholars lamented the lack of thorough studies of the relationships obtaining between Israelite and Judaean materials in the History; similarly, they also expressed interest in the passage of Israelite materials into Judah. It was likewise felt that more sure criteria must be derived for distinguishing the DtrG stratum, and in this connexion some scholars suggested that motif analyses and redaction critical studies would prove helpful tools.

The related questions of a more precise determination of the character of P and the relationship between D and P were also expressed in several groups: "is P in reality a Palestinian redaction of the fundamentally revolutionary theological conception of the Exile which is represented by the exilic D?" Do we have to do with a conflict between the Returnees and those who had remained in the land? And finally, is the theological paradigm consisting of "apostasy-punishment-restoration" a narrow Deuteronomistic axiom, or did it have a wider base in phenomena such as pre-exilic prophecy or in the work of Deutero-Isaiah?

This tendency of the discussion groups to concentrate on the problems centring on the Exile was also felt when subjects related to Israel's history and the history of Israelite religion were broached. It was pointed out that earlier research was concerned to present a sort of "maximal approach" to these two disciplines. This approach has usually entailed that scholars base their work on the understanding of history present in the Old Testament and on the Old Testament understanding of Israel's religious evolution, for only subsequently to adduce a concept of Israel's later development. Against this it was suggested that it is methodologically preferable in the first instance to confine oneself to a sort of "minimal approach", by which one begins around the period of the Exile, about which we are reasonably informed (i.e., via the great prophetic writings and the Deuteronomistic Historical Work). From this vantage, then, one would cautiously attempt to work backwards in order to arrive at an understanding of the religious and historical relations of earlier periods. In this fashion we might be able to avoid the pitfall of the apologetic attitude which has characterized recent attempts at historical reconstruction. Thus we would presumably be able to offer a more adequate picture of the entire development, so that we shall have a better foundation when we attempt traditio-historical work with the texts and investigate both the milieu in which they arose and were transmitted as well as the functions they exercised in their social and religious milieux. In any case, it is clear that future accounts of Israel's history by Scandinavian tradition historians will mark a departure from the classical histories.

It was significant that the history of religions as such played only a modest role in the discussions that were held at Sandbjerg. This is striking when we consider the role played by the history of religions in Scandinavian research until very recently. In this connexion it is sufficient to mention the series of treatments dealing with sacral kingship which appeared after Engnell's doctoral dissertation was published (1943) and the not inconsiderable number of studies of Israelite religion which the publication of the Ugaritic materials made possible (eg., Hvidberg 1938, Pedersen 1940, and Hammershaimb 1945 and 1960). In contrast with scholars' earlier willingness to adumbrate sharply defined pictures of the development of Israelite religion, the discussion groups evinced rather more caution and hesitation. To take but a single example, it is noteworthy that most researchers would no longer regard sacral kingship as the central institution and thus the central religious motif in Israelite religion. It appears that the extraordinary emphasis on sacral kingship somewhat overrated a specifically Jerusalemite phenomenon, whose significance was limited outside of Jerusalem itself. With Isaiah as the sole Jerusalemite prophet, and with the Psalms, which we only possess in their Jerusalemite form, as point of departure, the motif of sacral kingship has achieved more prominence than it deserves, a fact which naturally is also a result of the adoption of the Messianic tradition by the Church.

If one of the foci of the discussions was Deuteronomism, the other was probably prophetism. In this respect the symposium seems to have reflected a general tendency in Old Testament research. Here, too, the problems associated with the final redaction and written fixation took pride of place. Once again the special problems presented by the Exile were drawn into the debate. How much actually happened to the prophetic traditions during the process of tradition — possibly in oral form — and how much happened to them in the course of redaction? To what extent did the crisis of the Exile bring about reinterpretation of old prophetic traditions, and in what way did the theological and religious reflections of the exiles leave their mark on the final assembly and combination of these traditions? Is it possible to distinguish sharply between those traditions which may be reasonably assigned to the prophetic circles of the 8th and 7th centuries and those which were the objects of "creative new- or post-interpretation" during the Exile? As in the discussion of Deuteronomism, scholars once again raised the problem of the relationship between the Northern and Southern Kingdoms, or, rather, between Jerusalem on the one hand and the provinces on the other. Such tensions were felt to underlie a number of prophetic traditions. Is it possible to speak of points of contact between such Judaean prophets as Amos and Micah and pre-Deuteronomistic circles in the Northern Kingdom, that is, connexions which bypass Jerusalem? And if so, does not this fact imply that it is an oversimplification to regard the connexion between Deuteronomism and prophetism as a mere matter of Deuteronomistic redaction and interpolation of earlier prophetic writings?

The Psalms did not play a major role in the discussions held at Sandbjerg. In part, this is explained by the religio-historical observations offered above, but it is also in part explained by the external technical circumstance that the address on the Psalms was delivered on the last day of the symposium and was not followed by group discussion. But it should also be added that Mowinckel's fundamental studies of the Psalms from the 1920's represent that part of Scandinavian research in the first half of this century which has best been able to stand the test of time.

As we have indicated above, traditio-historical research in Scandinavia is in process of transformation. The main question is as to whether the Scandinavian inheritance from the first two-thirds of the century provides a sound basis for completing the transformation. Alternatively, is it possible that the distinctive views of our predecessors and teachers actually impede further progress? Will we be able to learn from their openness with respect to the difficulties and their ability to see new solutions, so that their contributions will remain an inspiration to seek new pathways, or will they inhibit our development? It was with questions of this sort that we were concerned to grapple in the course of the Sandbjerg symposium, and it was indeed encouraging to discover that new developments are already under way which do not indicate a complete break with the past.

NOTES

The Traditio-historical Study of the
Pentateuch since 1945, with special
Emphasis on Scandinavia

This paper was first published in *Law, History, and Tradition*. Selected Essays
by Eduard Nielsen, København 1983, pp. 138-154.

1. I have touched on this subject previously in a lecture addressed to Viden-
   skabernes Selskab 21. Jan. 1982, under the title, "Northern Provenience
   of Tradition-material in the Pentateuch".
2. This view is systematically presented in his commentary on Genesis (1949-
   1952).
3. Cf. H.S. Nyberg: Our Old Testament is mainly, in its written form, post-
   exilic (see 1935, p. 8).
4. I should like to mention that I returned from a brief study-voyage to
   Uppsala in 1947 not only having received enduring inspiration to work
   with the texts from new points of view, but also the richer for a friendship
   that lasted as long as Engnell lived, in spite of the fact that his influence
   diminished as I made acquaintance with the works of von Rad and M.
   Noth. These combined forces influenced my University Prize Essay on
   "The Significance of Oral Tradition for the Evolution of the Old Testament, with Emphasis on the Pentateuch". My essay later appeared as a
   number of articles in DTT (1950-52), and subsequently as *Oral Tradition*
   (1954), a declaration of war which, I fear, has brought me some notoriety
   in the world of Continental Old Testament studies. Again, reinforced by
   the study of half a score articles and monographs by A. Alt, these influences expressed themselves even more strongly in my work on Shechem
   (1955).
   It has always given me pleasure to attempt to trace the growth of traditions
   and their interrelationships in order to conceive more or less plausible explanations of the fact that the textual evolution has resulted in the texts
   as we now have them. This fondness has also characterized more recent
   works from my hand, perhaps with a tendency to develop working hypotheses that appeal too much to the imagination: at any rate, it has not
   always been overly difficult for my critics to unravel them again.
5. That is, it was a formative stage for the historical writing that began with
   the Monarchy.
6. And perhaps Gen 23, the story of the purchase of the cave of Machpelah,
   as well. The literary critics are still in doubt as to whether Gen 23 belongs
   to P.
7. I note with pleasure that in his address to the conference in Vienna Magne
   Sæbø definitely affirms that the Priestly Writing was also a legal collec-

tion, characterized by interest in cultic-ritual matters, and in the procla-
mation of law in general (Sæbø 1981).

8. With his work *Bundestheologie im Alten Testament* (1969), in which
    he emphasized the striking silence in the older pre-exilic literature concer-
    ning the covenant between Yahweh and Israel.

9. Already when I was a student my teacher Fl. Hvidberg called attention
    to the resemblance (around 1945).

10. Whose Edinburgh address (Rendtorff 1975) is referred to by Schmid.

Remarks of an outsider concerning
Scandinavian Tradition History with
Emphasis on the Davidic Traditions

A shorter German version of this paper entitled "Die skandinavische traditionsgeschichtliche Forschung. Am Beispiel der Davidsüberlieferungen" was published
in *Glaube und Gerechtigkeit*. Rafael Gyllenberg in memoriam, Helsinki 1983,
pp. 47-68.

1. Cf. Engnell 1945, pp. 188f, 209; 1962-63 II, col. 715; cf. also Ringgren 1969, p. x.
2. Compare the remarks of Nyberg 1972, p. 10; and those of Knight 1973, pp. 292-295.
3. Cf. Engnell 1945, p. 11; further, Ringgren 1969, p. ix.
4. Knight offers a useful survey of Scandinavian traditio-historical research in the second half of his above-cited dissertation (1973, pp. 215-399), where Engnell figures as "The Center of the Debate" (pp. 260-295).
5. Cf. Engnell 1960, p. 23; 1969, pp. 5f; and Nyberg 1972, p. 9; Knight 1973, pp. 219.260. – NB Engnell 1969, pp. 3-11 = 1962-63 II, cols. 1254-1261.
6. Cf. Engnell 1960, p. 23; 1969, pp. 7-9.66; NB Engnell 1969, pp. 50-76 = 1962-63 II, cols. 152-165.
7. Cf. Engnell 1960, pp. 20f; 1969, p. 9f.
8. On Mowinckel's position with regard to the then-contemporary controversy, see Knight, 1973, pp. 251f.
9. Cf. 1969, p. 11. Engnell's all-encompassing use of the term "tradition history" is also illustrated by the fact that he subtitled his account of the Old Testament, *Gamla Testamentet* (1945), "a traditio-historical introduction".
10. To Engnell's use of the terms "analysis" and "synthesis" should be compared the remarks of Ringgren 1966, cols. 647f.
11. Engnell 1969, pp. 12-34 = 1962-63 II, cols. 708-723.
12. Engnell 1969, pp. 180-184 = 1962-63 II, cols. 336-340.
13. Evidence is virtually discoverable at will in all of Engnell's writings. According to Ringgren the attention paid to "ideological factors" is a significant aspect of Engnell's traditio-historical method (1969, p. x).
14. In this connexion see Carlson 1962, which literally teems with the expressions "idea, ideology, ideological".
15. Knight remarks that Ringgren has made "the entire proof-sheets for the second volume" available to him; these, however, did not comprise more than 107 pages (Knight 1973, p. 261, n. 5).
16. Cf. Engnell 1962-63 I, col. 404; 1969, p. 40. NB Engnell 1969, pp. 35-49 = 1962-63 I, cols. 762-773.
17. Engnell 1969, pp. 215-236 = 1962-63 II, cols. 77-91.

18. Cf. Engnell 1945, pp. 221.224.226f; 1969, p. 42.

19. Cf. Engnell 1962-63 I, col. 402; 1969, pp. 81-85.

20. According to his preface, Ahlström's work is "the fruit of an inspirational path of research" founded by Engnell; moreover, Ahlström claims that it is "not only extremely fruitful, but in many respects represents a complete renewal of our discipline". Carlson's book is dedicated to the memory of Engnell, and, according to Knight he follows Engnell's programme more faithfully than any other (Knight 1973, p. 327). The priority in this respect must rather be accorded to Ahlström.

21. See also the subtitle of his book, "Eine Liturgie aus dem Ritual des leidenden Königs".

22. On Engnell see the lengthy article on the Psalms, 1969, pp. 68-122 = 1962-63 II, cols. 618-656.

23. Cf. Ps. 79:2.10; 90:13.16; 102:15.29 for the former term, and Ps. 30:5; 50:5; 52:11; 85:9; 132:9.16, among others, for the latter.

24. This and the following questions are more extensively discussed in Veijola's book on Ps. 89 (1982).

25. The average length of the stichoi in the hymnic part (v. 2-3. 6-19) is 16,16 consonants, while in the divine oracle (v. 20b-38) and subsequent lament (v. 39-46) it is only 13,03 consonants. In the concluding petition (v. 47-52) this figure again rises to 16,42 consonants per stichos.

26. On the promise to David as a "covenant", see 2 Sam 23:5; Isa 55:3; Jer 33:21; 2 Chr 13:5; 21:7 (cf. also 2 Chr 7:18); and on the "election" of the king, see Deut 17:15; 1 Sam 10:24; 16:8.9.10; 2 Sam 6:21; 1 Kgs 8:16; 11:34; Hag 2:23; Ps 78:70. For an evaluation, cf. Veijola 1982, pp. 67-69.

27. Ps 2 (v. 10); 14 (v. 2); 36 (v. 4); 47 (v. 8), and the actual maśkil-psalms 32; 42; 44; 45; 52-55; 74; 78; 88; 89 are mentioned in this connexion; of these, only Ps 78 is excluded from the New Year Festival on the grounds that it is a didactic psalm (Ahlström, pp. 21-26).

28. Ahlström (pp. 164-169) concludes that a divinity named Dod was worshipped in Israel on the basis of Amos 8:14; Cant 5:9; 1 Sam 10:14-16 (!), and the stele of Mesha (where a divine epithet dwd appears in line 12).

29. Ahlström's remark (p. 16) that Gunkel had termed this psalm a hymn is quite misleading. On Gunkel's characterization of the Gattungen in Ps 89, see Veijola 1982, p. 18.

30. Hymnic elements are rather the rule than the exception in the collective lament; cf. Ps 44:2-4; 74:13-17; 80:2.9-12; Isa 63:7.14; Micah 7:18-20; further, see Gunkel 1933, pp. 134f.

31. It is out of the question to translate this phrase in the present tense (against Ahlström 1959, pp. 98f., who translates "now you speak ... ").

32. Indeed, among others this view was entertained by F. Hitzig, R. Smend, Th. Cheyne, E. Reuss, R. Kraetzschmar, J. Wellhausen, F. Buhl, F. Baethgen, and somewhat later by the Swede, S. Linder (see Veijola 1982, p. 133, n. 1).

33. The collective tendency of Ps 89 is no isolated phenomenon; rather, it corresponds to the general trend of the late-exilic reception of the Davidic theology, as I have attempted to show (1982, pp. 133-173).
34. On the use of the number seven, cf. Carlson 1964, pp. 151.154f.163.166. 176.202.204, and the contact to the Krt-text, pp. 67.144.190f.
35. It is not always easy to make out what Carlson regards as Deuteronomistic (see below). In the following passages in the Books of Samuel he assumes a more or less clear Deuteronomistic influence: 1 Sam 2:27-36 (p. 44); 4:4 (p. 72); 8 (p. 32); 9:16 (p. 53); LXX 10:1 (p. 53); 12 (p. 32); 13:14 (p. 53); 25:24-31 (p. 47, n.3); 26:17-25 (pp. 47.208f); 2 Sam 1:18 (p. 48); 2:1 (p. 41); 2:8-11 (p. 50); 3:2-5 (p. 50); 4:2b-3 (p. 51); 5:2 (p. 53); 5:4-5 (p. 55); 5:12 (pp. 57.119); 6:21 (pp. 53.94); 7 (p. 104); 8:1 (p. 41); 10:1 (p. 41); 11:21 (p. 150); 12:1-14 (pp. 156-160); 12:24b β-25 (p. 161, n.3); 13:1 (p. 41); 15:1 (p. 41); 15:24-29 (p. 174); 17:14 (p. 169); 18:18 (p. 187); 21:2b (p. 200, n. 3); 21:7 (p. 200, n. 3); 21:18 (p. 41); 24:1b (p. 213); 24:3-4b (p. 205); 24:10 (pp. 207f.); 24:11-14 (pp. 211-213); 24:17 (p. 217, n. 2).
36. Cf. Engnell 1945, pp. 231-247; Carlson 1962.
37. Cf. Engnell 1962-63 II, col. 870; Ahlström 1959, p. 53 (without evidence); Carlson 1964, pp. 23.30-32; 1962, col. 416.
38. So, for example, 1 Sam 2:27-36 (Carlson 1964, p. 45) and 2 Sam 4:2b-3 (p. 51 and n. 2).
39. Mettinger makes a not unimportant correction to the views offered in 1976 in his most recent work (1982), p. 49 and n. 41, where he allows that v. 13 does not belong to the ancient oracle, but to its Deuteronomistic revision.
40. Both scholars emphasize the considerable unity of the Deuteronomistic circle and the impossibility of distinguishing various stages in its activity (Engnell 1945, p. 245; 1962-63, II, col. 870; Carlson 1964, pp. 22-24; 1962).
41. Yet another pre-existent element in 2 Sam 7 was the veto against construction of the Temple (v. 1a. *2-5), which DtrH connected with the dynastic promise (Veijola 1975, pp. 72-77, and the supplement to this, 1982, pp. 62-65).
42. Grønbæk only accepts Deuteronomistic influence in the following passages: 1 Sam 15:2; 30:21-25 (?); 2 Sam 1:17-18 (p. 222) and 1:19-27 in its present context; 2:10a.11; 5:4-5.11-12.13-16, and in the transposition of 5:17-25, which he holds originally followed 5:1-3.
43. On 1 Sam 16:1-13, cf. Veijola 1982, pp. 70-72.
44. Thus, for example, in 1 Sam 20:12-17.42b; 23:16-18; 24:18-23a; 25:28-30; 2 Sam 3:28-29; 4:4 (cf. 2 Sam 9).
45. Cf. Grønbæk 1971, pp. 75.79.91.94f.125.145.155.220.
46. 1 Sam 16:1-13 is supposed to be based on Ps 89:20-21 (sic!), while 1 Sam 21:11-16 relies on Ps 34.

47. However, in my opinion 1 Kgs 1:35 is secondary, i.e., Deuteronomistic (Veijola 1975, pp. 17.26-28; nevertheless, Mettinger 1976, p. 29 and n. 10, argues against this, but I remain unconvinced). Langlamet, too, sees 1 Kgs 1:35 as secondary, though pre-Deuteronomistic (1976, pp. 494-498.528).

48. Among the Davidic traditions in the historical books, Mettinger (1976) explicitly takes the following passages to be Deuteronomistic: 1 Sam 23:16-18 (?) (p. 37); 24:18-23a (?) (p. 37); 25:32-34.39a (p. 36); 2 Sam 3:28-29. 38-39 (p. 29); 7:1b.10-11a.22b-26 (p. 62); 8:1a.14b-15, and the whole of ch. 8 in its present context (p. 41); 12:7b-10 or 12:7b-12 (p. 30); 17:5-14 (p. 29); 21:7 (?) (p. 38).

49. Würthwein 1974, pp. 11-17; Veijola 1975, pp. 18.25; Langlamet 1976, pp. 330-337.482-528.

50. From an undated letter of Gressmann, cited from Klatt 1969, p. 74.

51. According to Richter (1971, pp. 156f), these are the indispensable presuppositions of the study of traditions.

Tradition and History, with Emphasis
on the Composition of the Book of Joshua

1. Engnell presented his guidelines in *Gamla Testamentet I* (1945). See also *A Rigid Scrutiny* (1969) in which some of the most important articles in *Svenskt Bibliskt Uppslagsverk* (2nd ed. 1962-63) are found in English translation. Cf. the article by Timo Veijola, notes 5, 6, 11, 12, 16, 17.
2. Engnell's *Gamla Testamentet II* was intended to realize this analysis in detail. Although Engnell never published this work, its materials are surely present in the various articles on the individual books of the OT in *SBU*.
3. At this time there were some exegetical "heavyweights" in Scandinavia, figures such as Johs. Pedersen, S. Mowinckel, H.S. Nyberg, and Johs. Lindblom, who paved the way for new approaches.
4. Engnell's views on the relation between oral and written tradition are presented in his article entitled "Gamla Testamentet" in 1962-63 I, cols. 750ff. An animated discussion concerning the significance of oral tradition was occasioned by G. Widengren (1959). Widengren is strongly critical of Engnell's understanding of the significance of oral tradition. However, in the study of the prophets the idea nevertheless came to play a significant role; cf. H.S. Nyberg (1935), and E. Nielsen (1954).
5. The notices at Deut 17:18 and 2 Macc 19:20 are significant in this connexion.
6. Engnell denied any dependence on M. Noth, who had claimed (1943, pp. 53ff) that there was no Deuteronomistic redaction in Gen-Num. While admitting that he was familiar with Noth's study, Engnell (1945, p. 210, n. 3) stated that he in fact had merely developed further ideas already published by Aa. Bentzen (1941, p. 46).
7. The concept of "D" in its broad sense meant to Engnell a designation for the community or circle, the "D group", who were responsible for the composition of the "D Work", stretching from Deut to 2 Kgs. The final phase of redaction was not especially characterized. I have adopted the designation "Dtr" to signify the final stage of the redactional and creative activity of the strongly nationalistic and Mosaically orientated "literary" activity of the D group. However, the idea of the restoration of the Davidic empire will naturally not have been the especial property of the D group. The same notion is detectable in the geographical scheme of the P Work and in the prophetic books (cf. Carlson 1966). The idea of the reunification of the Divided Monarchy will certainly have been topical during the reign of king Rehoboam; nevertheless it was probably first in the years subsequent to 722 BC, when the punishment was apparent to all, that an ideology of the sort promulgated by the D group and Dtr will have gained momentum. Cf. Weinfeld 1972.
8. Cf. Exod 32:11/Jos 7:7. I should like to express my thanks to E. Aurelius of the University of Lund for calling my attention to this.

9.   S. Tengström (1976, pp. 149ff, esp. pp. 152ff) believes that although the
     proto-Deuteronomistic material in Jos 8:30-35 is fragmentary, it never-
     theless formed the basis for Deut 27:5-7.

10. The most recent major investigation of the traditions in the Book of Jos-
     hua is E. Otto (1975a). Otto follows a literary-critical method and divides
     the text up into a Source A and a Source B, of which the last-named large-
     ly corresponds to my Dtr. According to Otto, Source A is "a part of the
     Jahwistic History which is connected to Num 32" (p. 103), and derives
     from Gilgal. He further maintains that the traditions were attached to
     Gilgal because of the historical developments during the era of Saul and
     David. Some of these materials will originally have belonged in Gilgal,
     while others, such as the Shiloh traditions, were eventually attached to
     Gilgal as a result of David's conscious policy of linking the Northern
     Kingdom to Judah. Otto's Source A includes my P materials, of which the
     pre-priestly materials are the essence. I am unable to agree with Otto's
     surgical procedures, however.

11. The concept of text structure is here used of a section of text which is
     organized in such a way that the events described follow important data
     within the Mosaic salvation history. Similar structures have been observed
     by, among others, A. Schmitt (1977). Structural comparison has been
     shown to be a useful method by H. Kimura (1981, pp. 29ff) in the demon-
     stration of correspondences between the Elijah (1 Kgs 19) and Isaiah (ch.
     6) traditions.

12. This is a truth requiring some modifications, since the covenant between
     the scouts and Rahab in Jos 2 must be characterized as a transgression; cf.
     Exod 23:32; Deut 7:2. A literary-critical analysis of these texts, as well as
     a traditio-historical evaluation of the relationship between them is offered
     by E. Otto (1975a, pp. 203ff). Otto feels that these texts, taken together
     with Exod 34:11b-16, are dependent upon a common *Vorlage* (p. 223).

13. Cf. Num 21:1-3, where the struggle against the king of Arad is related in
     a sequence consisting of defeat-promise-victory-consecration to destruc-
     tion-placename aetiology. It should also be noted that both tell ʾarad and
     et-tell flowered in EB II, and were rebuilt during the Iron Age.

14. On this sort of border description, cf. Sæbø 1974 and 1978.

15. This verse requires more detailed analysis; however, its context simply
     seems to suggest that the verse describes the area in which Israelites, Phi-
     listines, and Aramaeans dwell. Yahweh has also directed *their* history.
     "Cushites" here signifies the "barbarians", that is, the peoples who dwel-
     led outside of the area and of whom Yahweh – for that reason – dis-
     approved.

16. Here we ought perhaps to recall that in Gen 28:10 Jacob is only a few
     hundred metres from the place "between Bethel and Ai", at which Abra-
     ham (Gen 13) and Joshua (Jos 8:1ff) are also reported. The phraseology
     in Gen 13:14 and 28:14 corresponds. However, in the Book of Joshua,
     Dtr has not the slightest interest in relating the pre-eminent sanctuary of

the Northern Kingdom to Joshua, the prototype of the ideal Jerusalemite king.

17. My hypothesis is that the conquests of Joshua listed in Jos 10-12 actually reflect David's war in Cis-Jordan, about which we are not informed elsewhere. Cf. Ahlström 1980.

18. As I shall attempt to explain below, I believe that the P groups, that is, the priests at the local sanctuaries, both preserved and at least to some extent linguistically formed these materials before Dtr took possession of them.

19. Cf. Hammershaimb 1977; Ringgren 1977. The complete publication of the texts was undertaken by J. Hoftijzer and G. van der Kooij 1976.

20. Thus the Samaritan Pentateuch, the Peshittta, and the Vulgate. On the discussion concerning Balaam's place of origin, see now H.-P. Müller (1978, p. 61).

21. The city-state of Jerusalem (*māt Urušalim*) will surely have extended over a considerable part of the habitations in the Judaean mountains. The opposition between the south and the north was already present in the Amarna period; Lab'ayu, the king of Shechem, controlled the region between Jerusalem and Gezer.

22. This is a conclusion which I have found irresistable (1969, p. 73).

23. The work will appear in 1985 and has the provisional title *Conquest and Allotment. Studies on the Book of Joshua.*

24. David was the first "southerner" to organize such a state, using Jerusalem as his power-base. Although Jerusalem lay far from the major caravan routes, the city succeeded in retaining its influence over the centuries not only because of religious reasons, but also because of topography. The extended ridges which were surrounded by deep valleys were well suited for development towards the north. This happened by stages on both the southeastern and western heights by the utilization of east-west orientated depressions in the bedrock. See Ottosson 1981a, pp. 6f.

Selected Aspects of Nordic Traditio-historical
Psalm Research since Engnell: Limitations and
Possibilities

1. On Sigmund Mowinckel's significance as a student of psalms, see eg. Kapel-
    rud 1966, pp. 65-81, and 1967; Ap-Thomas 1966. From a form critical
    point of view see Gerstenberger 1974. On Mowinckel's conception of the
    cult and its possible contemporary significance cf. Otto 1975b.
2. Cf. Engnell 1945 and 1962-63. Cf. the article above by Ottosson, note 1.
3. From, among others, Nyberg, on the dominant importance of the oral tra-
    dition; cf. Engnell 1945, pp. 28ff, and esp. pp. 39ff; on H.S. Nyberg see
    Knight 1973, pp. 233ff. Further, Engnell also received impulses from
    S.H. Hooke (1933 and 1935) and others concerning sacral kingship and its
    cultic functions in the ancient Near East; cf. Engnell 1943, p. 2 *et passim.*
4. Engnell's acceptance of Mowinckel's view is emphasized by Engnell (1945,
    p. 52, and esp. 1953, p. 86).
5. Among many similar attestations see Mowinckel's thorough and lasting
    concern with Engnell's hypotheses in 1951; otherwise see eg. Ringgren
    1966, cols. 645f, and Rendtorff 1966, pp. 5f.
6. This is an extremely important point for Engnell (see above, n. 4). How-
    ever, this does not mean that Engnell believes that every psalm is *a priori*
    to be regarded as a cultic text, but rather that most of them have on exa-
    mination proved to be such, or that it has to be investigated, whether
    they are best interpreted in this light (cf. 1962-63 II, col. 643).
7. In the second edition of *SBU* (1962-63) these distinctions are detectable
    in the words emphasized below in italics: "From the point of view of trans-
    mission the psalms of the Psalter *possibly* enjoy an unusual position, in
    that we should *probably* assume that in actuality they were written down
    at a very early stage" (II, cols. 621f).
8. The view was already sketched out in Engnell's article in 1948-52 II,
    col. 792. Local Yahweh cults, as is well known, are currently being sought
    by the archeologists. In this connexion, it may be of interest to note that
    the burial inscription of the singer Uri-Yahu (in Kirbet el-Qôm around the
    middle of the 8th cent.) may possibly represent such a local Yahweh cult
    with a living psalm tradition (see below n. 17). On the question of a
    local Yahweh cult in Kuntillet 'Ajrud, cf. Meshel 1977, pp. 272f.
9. Cf. 1962-63 II, col. 1257: the written fixation of the psalms served in part
    as a "support for the memory".
10. On this subject Knight 1973, pp. 267f. 289. As late as in his article entitled
    "Traditionshistorisk metod" (1962-63 II, col. 1256), Engnell wrote without
    reservations: "Not only the lesser units, but also the great complexes,
    or indeed whole collections or works of tradition, will have been fixed
    already at the stage of oral tradition, which is why the written fixation did
    not entail anything revolutionarily new."
11. The Asaph-psalms (1962-63 II, col. 626); Korah-psalms (col. 627) and the
    lamnaṣṣeᵃḥ psalms (cols. 631f). See further Illmann 1976, pp. 51f. Illmann

presents a number of very important objections to the hypothesis that the Asaph psalms derived from North Israel. He also contests the idea that they represent any form of specific self-contained tradition (pp. 59ff).

12. Engnell is also able to distinguish between the psalms' "formal character as royal psalms" and their conceivable "democratized", or "factual, actual use" (1962-63 II, col. 630). On the question of whether the psalms were at one and the *same* time used in a royal ideological and a "democratized" manner, see Holm Nielsen 1955, p. 138.

13. See above, n. 11. Engnell is also sceptical of the possibility of an Elohistic redaction of Ps 42-83, since, as he notes, the predominance of Elohim as a divine name could well be an original phenomenon connected with the "provenance and Sitz im Leben" of these psalms. See 1962-63 II, col. 620.

14. With some reservations, Ringgren points to the alternation between *ʿal* and *ʾel* in Ps 18/2 Sam 22:42 as deriving from "a weak pronunciation of *ʿayin*", i.e., from oral transmission (cf. p. 44). However, an arbitrary alternation of *ʿal* and *ʾel* may have been well established before *any* transmission of the psalm, so that we could hardly conclude that oral transmission was the cause here.

15. Here the date of Isa 9:1-6 is left open; cf. p. 199 (the historification of cultic psalms may have taken place already prior to the Exile).

16. Additions: Ps 22:30-32; 32:8-10; 51:20f; 81:7b-11. Post-exilic psalms: Ps 1; 112; 127; 73; 90; 19b.

17. Regardless of whether this function or role was cultic in the narrow sense, like the role of the divine king, or in a broad sense, i.e., even in private songs of praise or lamentation, as when the singer Uri-Yahu (mid 8th cent.) writes about himself at his future gravesite:. . . *ûmimmēṣar yôdē lᵉʾel ŝarᵉ-tô hôŝîᵃ lô*; in choice of words and content this is very close to a cultic act (cf. Ps 116:3; 118:5)! (On the text and its reading, see Mittmann 1981, pp. 144.146.

18. Note the distinction between the sacrificer and the patriarch in Deut 26:5ff; or between those who may fairly be designated cultic participants in Ps 78:8 and the generation of the desert in Ps 78:12ff. Further on the question of the actualization of history in the (cultic) psalms, see Kühlewein 1973.

19. This may also be expressed in Springer's monograph; on pp. 116f the possibility is mentioned that Ps 2 and 110 may have been parts of longer psalms. Some evidence is offered, but the author adds that, "This hypothesis is . . . unprovable".

20. On v. 6a, Springer notes that the mountains of the gods of Ugarit "are not . . . the place of initiation of earthly kings" (p. 115).

21. Against Norin, pp. 148f.151.112.114ff respectively. Cf. Davies 1981, p. 115.

22. Norin's hypothesis of a mythically-coloured Exodus poetic tradition lacks a middle term between late monarchical times and the so-called "Ur-Meeres-

lied", which Norin dates to the time of the events depicted, or up to a century later (pp. 92f, cf. 104f).

23. The presumed Ugaritic original will probably have referred to *mdbr qdš*, cf. *KTU* 1.23, 65. Ginsberg 1936, p. 130 and n. 1 seems not to be correct in supposing that this indicates the existence of a Kadesh oasis in Syria as well. The Ugaritic may rather refer to a sacred desert, but it must be held to be extremely likely that the *Israelites* read this passage in the psalm on Kadesh-Barnea in early monarchical times.

24. On the other hand, I regard it as more uncertain when in this connexion Kapelrud finds a combination of Canaanite and Israelite in Ps 47:10, where "the name of Abraham is obviously substituted for another one", (i.e., a Canaanite name such as Elyon). As far as I can see the non-Canaanite element in Ps. 47:9-10 is that the rulership of the god over the *peoples* is stressed. I know of no certain indications of this perspective in the Ugaritic texts. Cf. further, Schmidt 1966, p. 92. If this is the case, it is difficult to speak of a Canaanite *Vorlage* for Ps 47:10.

25. Ljung 1978, esp. chs. E, J, and K. The texts in question are Ps 6; 18:2-7. 17-20; 28:1-7; 31:2c-9; 71:2-5. 9- 13. 22; 116:1-9, and 143. See also the examples below.

26. Unlike sections which are rich in formulaic language, the non-formulaic sections of psalms dealing with personal need and salvation can be dated to exilic/post-exilic times, when reinterpretation of the pre-exilic psalms took place; cf. pp. 110ff.

27. Culley hoped that his investigation would, among other things, reveal whether the Old Testament psalms contain indications that they were orally composed and transmitted literature. His conclusion in this connexion was very hesitant: "It can only be said that the psalms with high formulaic content may be oral formulaic compositions or come from a period very close to the time when oral formulaic composition was being practised" (1967, p. 114). William R. Watters has investigated and evaluated Culley's work and has concluded, as far as I can see correctly, that Culley has failed to demonstrate a single aspect of old Hebrew poetry which might imply that this poetry was orally composed (Watters 1976, p. 17). While it has been and remains an open question to what extent Serbo-Croatian oral techniques may be presupposed in Homeric poetry, Culley relatively uncritically transfers Indo-European oral techniques onto old Hebrew poetry (1967, pp. 18f).

28. Thus the test which Inger Ljung carries out in ch. E (pp. 20ff) in which her starting group is compared with the control group consisting of Ps 18, 69, 86, and 116 is *valid*: those formulas or formulaic systems which, according to Ljung, are "common to" the psalms of the control group, are all attested three or more times. And when Ljung enquires as to whether each individual psalm among the twenty-six numbers in the starting group has 1/3 or more of its formulaic materials in common with the formulaic materials which are "common to" the psalms of the control group, then the

number of formulas in the twenty-six psalms *falls* if one ignores formulas which are only attested twice. The fraction of formulaic materials in common with the control group will then merely *rise*.

29. If we then accorded Ps 143:1-4b the predicate "high number of formulas", this would suggest that verses 1-4b offer challenges and motivations (cf. Ljung 1978, p. 82), and thus would fit relatively well *into* the compositional pattern in question.

30. Mettinger here finds that the term *nāgīd* was originally a secular title which was "theologized" towards the end of the tenth century (pp. 158ff. 162ff), and that the anointing of the king was still a secular act in David's case (p. 201), but it was later understood religiously – from the time of Solomon and onwards (pp. 201ff). These datings are still open to discussion.

31. Thus Otto 1975b, p. 25, though hardly correctly. It is not, as Otto suggests, the Sitz im Leben of the psalms, but their *Gattungen* which are characterized in the way stated, while at the same time these *Gattungen* are expressly emphasized as cultic categories. Cf. Westermann 1961, p. 116.

BIBLIOGRAPHY AND INDEX

The bibliography encompasses all works mentioned in this volume; the numbers under each entry comprise the index and refer to the corresponding pages of the present book.

Ahlström 1959
    G.W. Ahlström, Psalm 89. Eine Liturgie aus dem Ritual des leidenden Königs, Lund 1959.
    Cf. pp. 36-41; 75; 112; 115; 138 (notes 20f, 27-29, 31); 139 (note 37).

Ahlström 1962
    G.W. Ahlström, Die Königsideologie in Israel. Ein Diskussionsbeitrag, ThZ 18 (1962), pp. 205-10.
    Cf. p. 37.

Ahlström 1980
    G.W. Ahlström, Another Moses Tradition, JNES 39 (1980), pp. 65-69.
    Cf. p. 143 (note 17).

Ap-Thomas 1966
    D.R. Ap-Thomas, An Appreciation of Sigmund Mowinckel's Contribution to Biblical Studies, JBL 85 (1966), pp. 315-25.
    Cf. p. 144 (note 1).

Arendt 1981
    Rudolph Arendt, Pagten og Loven, København 1981.
    Cf. p. 75.

Astour 1966
    M.C. Astour, Political and Cosmic Symbolism in Genesis 14 and in its Babylonian Sources, in: Biblical Motifs: Origins and Transformations, ed. A. Altmann, Cambridge Mass. 1966, pp. 65-112.
    Cf. p. 85.

Balla 1928
    Emil Balla, Gerechtigkeit Gottes: II. Im AT und Judentum, RGG, 2. Aufl., 1927-31, Bd. 2, Tübingen 1928, col. 1039.
    Cf. p. 76.

Baltzer 1960
    Klaus Baltzer, Das Bundesformular (WMANT 4), Neukirchen 1960.
    Cf. p. 22.

Becker 1966
    Joachim Becker, Israel deutet seine Psalmen. Urform und Neuinterpretation in den Psalmen (Stuttgarter Bibelstudien 18), Stuttgart 1966.
    Cf. p. 114.

Becker 1977
    Joachim Becker, Die kollektive Deutung der Königspsalmen, in: Theologie und Philosophie 52 (1977), pp. 561-78.
    Cf. p. 41.

Bentzen 1939

Aage Bentzen, Fortolkning til de gammeltestamentlige salmer, København 1939.
    Cf. pp. 75; 77.
Bentzen 1941

Aage Bentzen, Indledning til Det gamle Testamente, København 1941 (Eng. translation: Introduction to the Old Testament I-II, Copenhagen 1948-49).
    Cf. p. 141 (note 6).
Bentzen 1945

Aage Bentzen, Det sakrale kongedømme. Bemærkninger i en løbende diskussion om de gammeltestamentlige salmer (Festskrift udgivet af Københavns Universitet), København 1945.
    Cf. p. 112.
Bentzen 1947

Aage Bentzen, Der Tod des Beters in den Psalmen. Randbemerkungen zur Diskussion zwischen Mowinckel und Widengren, in: Festschrift Otto Eissfeldt . . . dargebracht, ed. J. Fück, Halle a.d. Saale 1947, 57-60.
    Cf. p. 112.
Bernhardt 1961

Karl-Heinz Bernhardt, Das Problem der altorientalischen Königsideologie im Alten Testament. Unter besonderer Berücksichtigung der Geschichte der Psalmenexegese dargestellt und kritisch gewürdigt (SupplVT 8), Leiden 1961.
    Cf. p. 33.
Beyerlin 1959

Walter Beyerlin, Die Kulttraditionen Israels in der Verkündigung des Propheten Micha (FRLANT 72), Göttingen 1959.
    Cf. pp. 79; 124.
Birkeland 1938

Harris Birkeland, Zum hebräischen Traditionswesen. Die Komposition der prophetischen Bücher des Alten Testaments (Avhandlinger utgitt av Det norske Videnskaps-Akademi i Oslo, II. Hist.-Filos. Klasse. 1938. No. 1), Oslo 1938.
    Cf. pp. 12; 54.
Blenkinsopp 1976

J. Blenkinsopp, The Structure of P, CBQ 38 (1976), pp. 275-92.
    Cf. p. 86.
Boecker 1964

Hans Jochen Boecker, Redeformen des Rechtslebens im Alten Testament (WMANT 14), Neukirchen 1964.
    Cf. p. 102.
Bright 1965

John Bright, Jeremiah. Introduction, Translation, and Notes (The Anchor Bible 21), New York 1965.
    Cf. p. 66.

Buss 1969
    M.J. Buss, The prophetic Word of Hosea. A Morphological Study (BeihZAW 111), Berlin 1969.
        Cf. pp. 63f.

Carlson 1962
    R.A. Carlson, Deuteronomistisk, Svenskt Bibliskt Uppslagsverk, 2. Uppl., I, Stockholm 1962, cols. 413-18.
        Cf. pp. 137 (note 14); 139 (notes 36f, 40).

Carlson 1964
    R.A. Carlson, David, the Chosen King. A Traditio-Historical Approach to the Second Book of Samuel, Stockholm 1964.
        Cf. pp. 36; 39; 41-46; 139 (notes 34f, 37f, 40).

Carlson 1966
    R.A. Carlson, Profeten Amos och Davidsriket, RoB 25 (1966),pp. 57-78.
        Cf. p. 141 (note 7).

Carlson 1977
    R.A. Carlson, P-prologen i Gen. 1:1-2:3, SEÅ 41-42 (1976-77), pp. 57-68.
        Cf. p. 18.

Carroll 1981
    Robert P. Carroll, From Chaos to Covenant. Uses of Prophecy in the Book of Jeremiah, London 1981.
        Cf. p. 66.

Culley 1967
    Robert C. Culley, Oral Formulaic Language in the Biblical Psalms (Near and Middle East Series, No. 4), Toronto 1967.
        Cf. pp. 119f; 146 (note 27).

Culley 1980
    Robert C. Culley, review: Ljung 1978, SEÅ 45 (1980), pp. 133-35.
        Cf. p. 119.

Davies 1981
    G.I. Davies, review: Norin 1977, VT 31 (1981), pp. 110-17.
        Cf. p. 145 (note 21).

Diestel 1860
    L. Diestel, Die Idee der Gerechtigkeit, vorzüglich im Alten Testamente, Jahrbücher für deutsche Theologie 5 (1860), pp. 173-253.
        Cf. p. 70.

Elat 1977
    Moshe Elat, Economic Relations in the Lands of the Bible (c. 1000-539 B.C.) (Hebrew), Jerusalem 1977.
        Cf. p. 101.

Engnell 1943
    Ivan Engnell, Studies in Divine Kingship in the Ancient Near East, Uppsala 1943.
        Cf. pp. 32; 35f; 107; 110; 131; 144 (note 3).

Engnell 1945

Ivan Engnell, Gamla Testamentet. En traditionshistorisk inledning, I, Stockholm 1945.

Cf. pp. 11; 15-18; 29f; 32; 35; 44; 54; 56; 83f; 107; 109-112; 137 (notes 1, 3, 9); 138 (note 18); 139 (notes 36, 40); 141 (notes 1, 6); 144 (notes 2-4).

Engnell 1947

Ivan Engnell, Profetia och tradition. Några synspunkter på ett gammaltestamentligt centralproblem, SEÅ 12 (1947), pp. 110-39.

Cf. pp. 54; 56.

Engnell 1948-52

See Engnell 1962-63.

Engnell 1953

Ivan Engnell, 'Planted by the Streams of Water'. Some Remarks on the Problem of the Interpretation of the Psalms as Illustrated by a Detail in Ps. I, in: Studia Orientalia Ioanni Pedersen ... dicata, Hauniae 1953, pp. 85-96.

Cf. pp. 112; 144 (note 4).

Engnell 1960

Ivan Engnell, Methodological Aspects of Old Testament Study, Congress Volume Oxford 1959 (SupplVT 7), Leiden 1960, pp. 13-30.

Cf. pp. 29-32; 60; 137 (notes 5-7).

Engnell 1962-63

Ivan Engnell, articles in Svenskt Bibliskt Uppslagsverk (1. uppl. 1948-52), 2. uppl., I-II, Stockholm 1962-63.

Cf. pp. 13; 35; 56-63; 81; 83f; 108-113; 137 (notes 5f, 11f, 16f); 138 (notes 19, 22); 139 (notes 37, 40); 141 (notes 1, 4); 144 (notes 2, 6-11); 145 (notes 12f).

Engnell 1969

Ivan Engnell, A Rigid Scrutiny. Critical Essays on the Old Testament, ed. by John T. Willis, with the collaboration of Helmer Ringgren, Nashville 1969 (under the title: Critical Essays on the Old Testament, London 1970).

Cf. pp. 18; 30f; 35; 40; 56; 137 (notes 5-7, 9, 11f, 16f); 138 (notes 18f, 22); 141 (note 1).

Fahlgren 1932

K.Hj. Fahlgren, ṣᵉdāḳā, nahestehende und entgegengesetzte Begriffe im Alten Testament, Uppsala 1932.

Cf. pp. 68; 73.

Franken 1967

H.J. Franken, Texts from the Persian Period from Tell Deir 'Allā, VT 17 (1967), pp. 480-81.

Cf. p. 103.

Friis 1975

Heike Friis, Eksilet og den israelitiske historieopfattelse, DTT 38 (1975), pp. 1-16.

Cf. p. 23.

Frye 1957
    Northrop Frye, Anatomy of Criticism. Four Essays, Princeton, 1957.
        Cf. p. 65.

Gerhardsson 1961
    Birger Gerhardsson, Memory and Manuscript. Oral Tradition and Written
    Transmission in Rabbinic Judaism and Early Christianity (Acta Semina-
    rii Neotestamentici Upsaliensis, 22), Uppsala 1961.
        Cf. p. 63.

Gerleman 1982
    Gillis Gerleman, Der "Einzelne" der Klage- und Dankpsalmen, VT 32
    (1982), pp. 33-49.
        Cf. p. 124.

Gerstenberger 1974
    E. Gerstenberger, Psalms I. History of Research and Development of
    Method, in: Old Testament Form Criticism, ed. J.H. Hayes (Trinity Uni-
    versity Monograph Series on Religion, II), San Antonio 1974.
        Cf. p. 144 (note 1).

Ginsberg 1936
    H.L. Ginsberg, The Ugarit Texts (Hebrew), Jerusalem 1936.
        Cf. p. 146 (note 23).

Glueck 1927
    Nelson Glueck, Das Wort ḥesed im alttestamentlichen Sprachgebrauche
    als menschliche und göttliche gemeinschaftsgemässe Verhaltungsweise
    (BeihZAW 47), Giessen 1927.
        Cf. pp. 70; 73.

Grelot 1966
    Pierre Grelot, Die Tradition – Quelle und Milieu der Schrift, Concilium 2
    (1966), pp. 745-56.
        Cf. p. 66.

Gressmann 1924
    Hugo Gressmann, Die Aufgaben der alttestamentlichen Forschung, ZAW
    42 (1924), 1-33.
        Cf. p. 50.

Grice 1975
    H.P. Grice, Logic and Conversation, in: Syntax and Semantics, Vol. 3:
    Speech Acts, ed. P. Cole and J.L. Morgan, New York 1975, pp.41-58.
        Cf. p. 110.

Grønbæk 1971
    Jakob H. Grønbæk, Die Geschichte vom Aufstieg Davids (1. Sam. 15 –
    2. Sam. 5). Tradition und Komposition (Acta Theologica Danica 10),
    Copenhagen 1971.
        Cf. pp. 36, 39, 46-48, 139 (notes 42, 45).

Grønbæk 1972
    Jakob H. Grønbæk, Traditionshistorie og litterærkritik. Et stadigt aktuelt
    indledningsproblem i Det gamle Testamentes historiske bøger, DTT
    35 (1972), 12-29.
        Cf. p. 18.

Gunkel 1933

Hermann Gunkel, Einleitung in die Psalmen. Die Gattungen der religi-
ösen Lyrik Israels. Zu Ende geführt von Joachim Begrich, Göttingen
1933.
   Cf. p. 138 (note 30).

Gyllenberg 1946

R. Gyllenberg, review: Engnell 1945, Teologinen Aikakauskirja 51
(1946), pp. 151-60.
   Cf. p. 33.

Haldar 1947

Alfred Haldar, Studies in the Book of Nahum (Uppsala Universitets Årsskrift 1946:7), Uppsala 1947.
   Cf. p. 59.

Hammershaimb 1945

E. Hammershaimb, Immanuelstegnet, DTT 8 (1945), pp. 223-44 (Eng.
translation: The Immanuel Sign, StTh 3 (1949), pp. 124-42. Also in:
Some Aspects of Old Testament Prophecy from Isaiah to Malachi, København 1966, pp. 9-28).
   Cf. p. 131.

Hammershaimb 1960

E. Hammershaimb, On the Ethics of the Old Testament Prophets, Congress Volume Oxford 1959 (SupplVT 7), Leiden 1960, pp. 75-101. Also
in: Some Aspects of Old Testament Prophecy from Isaiah to Malachi, København 1966, pp. 63-90.
   Cf. p. 131.

Hammershaimb 1977

E. Hammershaimb, De aramæiske indskrifter fra udgravningerne i Deir
'Allā, DTT 40 (1977), pp. 217-42.
   Cf. p. 143 (note 19).

Hempel 1938

Johannes Hempel, Das Ethos des Alten Testaments (BeihZAW 67), Berlin 1938.
   Cf. p. 76.

Hentschke 1957

Richard Hentschke, Die Stellung der vorexilischen Schriftpropheten zum
Kultus (BeihZAW 75), Berlin 1957.
   Cf. p. 79.

Hölscher 1942

Gustav Hölscher, Die Anfänge der hebräischen Geschichtsschreibung (Sit-
zungsber. der Heidelb. Akademie der Wiss. Phil.-hist. Kl. Jahrg. 1941/42.
Abh. 3), Heidelberg 1942.
   Cf. p. 12.

Hoftijzer and van der Kooij 1976

J. Hoftijzer and G. van der Kooij, Aramaic Texts from Deir 'Alla (Docu-
menta et Monumenta Orientis Antiqui 19), Leiden 1976.
   Cf. p. 143 (note 19).

Holm-Nielsen 1955
Svend Holm-Nielsen, Den gammeltestamentlige salmetradition, DTT 18 (1955), pp. 135-48; 193-215.
Cf. pp. 107; 112-115; 145 (notes 12, 15f).

Holm-Nielsen 1960a
Svend Holm-Nielsen, Hodayot. Psalms from Qumran (Acta Theologica Danica 2), Aarhus 1960.
Cf. p. 114.

Holm-Nielsen 1960b
Svend Holm-Nielsen, The Importance of Late Jewish Psalmody for the Understanding of Old Testament Psalmodic Tradition, StTh 14 (1960), pp. 1-53.
Cf. pp. 113-115.

Holm-Nielsen 1972
Svend Holm-Nielsen, De sidste årtiers salme- og profetforskning. Nogle synspunkter, DTT 35 (1972), pp. 30-46.
Cf. pp. 114f.

Hooke 1933
S.H. Hooke (ed.), Myth and Ritual. Essays on the Myth and Ritual of the Hebrews in Relation to the Culture Pattern of the Ancient East, London 1933.
Cf. pp. 15; 144 (note 3).

Hooke 1935
S.H. Hooke (ed.), The Labyrinth. Further Studies in the Relation between Myth and Ritual in the Ancient World, London 1935.
Cf. pp. 15; 144 (note 3).

Hornung 1966
E. Hornung, Geschichte als Fest. Zwei Vorträge zum Geschichtsbild der frühen Menschheit, Darmstadt 1966.
Cf. p. 125.

Hvidberg 1938
Flemming F. Hvidberg, Graad og Latter i Det gamle Testamente. En Studie i kanaanæisk-israelitisk Religion, København 1938 (Eng. translation: Weeping and Laughter in the Old Testament. A Study of Canaanite-Israelite Religion, Leiden-København 1962).
Cf. p. 131.

Illman 1976
Karl-Johan Illman, Thema und Tradition in den Asaf-Psalmen (Meddelanden från Stiftelsens för Åbo Akademi Forskningsinstitut, Nr. 13), Åbo 1976.
Cf. p. 144 (note 11).

Jacobsen 1917
Johannes Jacobsen, Den gammeltestamentlige Teologi. Til Brug ved Undervisning (mimeograferet), København (1917).
Cf. p. 71.

Kallai 1960

Z. Kallai, The Northern Boundaries of Judah (Hebrew), Jerusalem 1960.
Cf. p. 95.

Kallai 1978

Z.Kallai, Judah and Israel – A Study in Israelite Historiography, IEJ 28 (1978), pp. 251-61.
Cf. p. 95.

Kapelrud 1948

Arvid S. Kapelrud, Joel Studies (Uppsala Universitets Årsskrift 1948:4), Uppsala 1948.
Cf. p. 59.

Kapelrud 1964

Arvid S. Kapelrud, Some Recent Points of View on the Time and Origin of the Decalogue, StTh 18 (1964), pp. 81-90.
Cf. p. 22.

Kapelrud 1965

Arvid S. Kapelrud, Scandinavian Research in the Psalms after Mowinckel, ASTI 4 (1965), pp. 74-90.
Cf. p. 107.

Kapelrud 1966

Arvid S. Kapelrud, Die skandinavische Einleitungswissenschaft zu den Psalmen, Verk. u. Forsch. 11 (1966), p. 62-93.
Cf. pp. 107; 144 (note 1).

Kapelrud 1967

Arvid S. Kapelrud, Sigmund Mowinckel and Old Testament Study, ASTI 5 (1967), pp. 4-29 (repr. in: God and His Friends in the Old Testament, Oslo 1979, pp. 53-78).
Cf. p. 144 (note 1).

Kapelrud 1972

Arvid S. Kapelrud, Kultus som livsgrunnlag i det gamle Israel, NTT 73 (1972), pp. 187-99.
Cf. p. 125.

Kapelrud 1975

Arvid S. Kapelrud, The Message of the Prophet Zephaniah. Morphology and Ideas, Oslo 1975.
Cf. p. 64.

Kapelrud 1977'

Arvid S. Kapelrud, Tradition and Worship: The Role of the Cult in Tradition Formation and Transmission, in: Tradition and Theology in the Old Testament, ed. Douglas A. Knight, Philadelphia 1977, pp. 101-24.
Cf. pp. 115; 118f; 125; 146 (note 24).

Kautzsch 1881

Emil Kautzsch, Ueber die Derivate des Stammes ṣdq im alttestamentlichen Sprachgebrauch, Tübingen 1881.
Cf. pp. 68; 70; 79.

Kimura 1981
   Hiroshi Kimura, Is 6:1-9:6. A Theatrical Section of the Book of Isaiah (typewritten diss.), Uppsala 1981.
      Cf. p. 142 (note 11).

Klatt 1969
   W. Klatt, Hermann Gunkel. Zu seiner Theologie der Religionsgeschichte und zur Entstehung der formgeschichtlichen Methode (FRLANT 100), Göttingen 1969.
      Cf. p. 140 (note 50).

Knight 1973
   Douglas A. Knight, Rediscovering the Traditions of Israel. The Development of the Traditio-Historical Research of the Old Testament, with Special Consideration of Scandinavian Contributions (SBL Dissertation Series 9), Missoula, Montana 1973.
      Cf. pp. 18; 53; 107; 137 (notes 2, 4f, 8, 15); 138 (note 20); 144 (notes 3, 10).

Koch 1953
   Klaus Koch, ṣdq im Alten Testament. Eine traditionsgeschichtliche Untersuchung (ungedr. Diss.), Heidelberg 1953.
      Cf. pp. 68; 76-79.

Koch 1976
   Klaus Koch, ṣdq, gemeinschaftstreu/heilvoll sein, THAT II, München 1976, cols. 507-30.
      Cf. pp. 74f; 78.

Kühlewein 1973
   J. Kühlewein, Geschichte in den Psalmen (Calwer Theologische Monographien A 2), Stuttgart 1973.
      Cf. p. 145 (note 18).

Langlamet 1976
   F. Langlamet, Pour ou contre Salomon? La rédaction prosalomonienne de I Rois, I-II, RB 83 (1976), pp. 321-79; 481-528.
      Cf. p. 140 (notes 47, 49).

Lauha 1947a
   Aarre Lauha, Uusi vanhatestamentillinen koulukunta, Vartija 1947, pp. 60-63.
      Cf. p. 34.

Lauha 1947b
   Aarre Lauha, Några randanmärkningar till diskussionen om kungaideologien i Gamla Testamentet, SEÅ 12 (1947), pp. 183-91.
      Cf. p. 34.

Leivestad 1946
   Ragnar Leivestad, Guds straffende rettferdighet. En undersøkelse av Det Gamle Testamentes bruk av ordstammen ṢDQ om Jahwæ i forbindelse med dom og straff (Tilleggshefte til NTT), Oslo 1946.
      Cf. p. 73.

Lindblom 1962

> Joh. Lindblom, Prophecy in Ancient Israel, Oxford 1962.
>
> *Cf. p. 64.*

Ljung 1978

> Inger Ljung, Tradition and Interpretation. A Study of the Use and Application of Formulaic Language in the so-called Ebed YHWH-psalms (Coniectanea Biblica. Old Testament Series 12), Lund 1978.
>
> *Cf. pp. 115; 119-122; 146 (notes 25f, 28); 147 (note 29).*

Lohfink 1978

> N. Lohfink, *ḥāram*, ThWAT III, Stuttgart 1978, cols. 192-213.
>
> *Cf. p. 90.*

Lord 1960

> Albert B. Lord, The Singer of Tales, Cambridge Mass. 1960.
>
> *Cf. pp. 60; 121.*

Malamat 1979

> Abraham Malamat, Israelite Conduct of War in the Conquest of Canaan According to the Biblical Tradition, in: Symposia Celebrating the Seventy-Fifth Anniversary of the Founding of the American Schools of Oriental Research (1900-1975), ed. F.M. Cross, Cambridge Mass. 1979, pp. 35-55.
>
> *Cf. p. 94.*

Mendenhall 1954a

> George E. Mendenhall, Ancient Oriental and Biblical Law, BA 17 (1954), 26-46 (repr. in: Law and Covenant in Israel and the Ancient Near East, Pittsburgh 1955).
>
> *Cf. p. 22.*

Mendenhall 1954b

> George E. Mendenhall, Covenant Forms in Israelite Tradition, BA 17 (1954), 50-76 (repr. in: Law and Covenant in Israel and the Ancient Near East, Pittsburgh 1955).
>
> *Cf. p. 22.*

Meshel 1977

> Z. Meshel, Kuntilet-Ajrud (Nord Sinaï), RB 84 (1977), pp. 270-73.
>
> *Cf. p. 144 (note 8).*

Mettinger 1976

> Tryggve N.D. Mettinger, King and Messiah. The Civil and Sacral Legitimation of the Israelite Kings (Coniectanea Biblica. Old Testament Series 8), Lund 1976.
>
> *Cf. pp. 36; 39; 45; 47-50; 124; 139 (note 39); 140 (notes 47f); 147 (note 30).*

Mettinger 1982

> Tryggve N.D. Mettinger, The Dethronement of Sabaoth. Studies in the Shem and Kabod Theologies (Coniectanea Biblica. Old Testament Series 18), Lund 1982.
>
> *Cf. p. 139 (note 39).*

Mittmann 1981

> S. Mittmann, Die Grabinschrift des Sängers Uriahu, ZDPV 97 (1981), pp. 139-52.
>
> *Cf. p. 145 (note 17).*

Mowinckel 1921
Sigmund Mowinckel, Psalmenstudien I. Åwän und die individuellen Kla-
gepsalmen (Videnskapsselskapets Skrifter. II. Hist.-Filos. Klasse 1921.
No. 4), Kristiania 1921.
Cf. p. 107.

Mowinckel 1922
Sigmund Mowinckel, Psalmenstudien II. Das Thronbesteigungsfest Jah-
wäs und der Ursprung der Eschatologie (Videnskapsselskapets Skrifter.
II. Hist.-Filos. Klasse 1921. No. 6), Kristiania 1922.
Cf. pp. 72f; 77; 107; 114;

Mowinckel 1927
Sigmund Mowinckel, Le Décalogue, Paris 1927.
Cf. p. 12.

Mowinckel 1928
Sigmund Mowinckel, Hypostasen, RGG, 2. Aufl. 1927-31, Bd. 2, 1928,
cols. 2065-2068.
Cf. p. 74.

Mowinckel 1929
Sigmund Mowinckel, Oversettelsen av 2. Mosebok kap. 1-24 og 32-34;
4. Mosebok 20-25 og 32-33 og 5. Mosebok, in: Det gamle Testamente
oversatt av S. Michelet, Sigmund Mowinckel og N. Messel, I, Loven eller
de fem Mosebøker, Oslo 1929.
Cf. p. 12.

Mowinckel 1930a
Sigmund Mowinckel, Bil'amsagnet, dets opkomst og dets utvikling, Edda
30 (1930), pp. 191-255.
Cf. p. 12.

Mowinckel 1930b
Sigmund Mowinckel, Der Ursprung der Bil'amsage, ZAW 48 (1930),
pp. 233-71.
Cf. p. 12.

Mowinckel 1942
Sigmund Mowinckel, Oppkomsten av profetlitteraturen, NTT 43 (1942),
pp. 65-111.
Cf. p. 55.

Mowinckel 1946
Sigmund Mowinckel, Prophecy and Tradition. The Prophetic Books in
the Light of the Study of the Growth and History of the Tradition (Av-
handlinger utgitt av Det norske Videnskaps-Akademi i Oslo, II. Hist.-
Filos. Klasse. 1946. No. 3), Oslo 1946.
Cf. p. 54.

Mowinckel 1947
Sigmund Mowinckel, Natanforjettelsen 2 Sam. kap. 7, SEÅ 12 (1947),
220-29.
Cf. p. 39.

Mowinckel 1951
Sigmund Mowinckel, Offersang og sangoffer. Salmediktningen i Bibelen,
Oslo 1951 (Eng. Translation: The Psalms in Israel's Worship, I-II, Oxford

1962).
   Cf. pp. 112; 118; 144 (note 5).
Mowinckel 1960
   Sigmund Mowinckel, review: Ahlström 1959, JSS 5 (1960), pp. 291-98.
   Cf. pp. 37; 41.
Mowinckel 1964a
   Sigmund Mowinckel, Erwägungen zur Pentateuch-quellenfrage, NTT 65
   (1964), pp. 1-136.
   Cf. pp. 12; 14.
Mowinckel 1964b
   Sigmund Mowinckel, Tetrateuch – Pentateuch – Hexateuch. Die Berich-
   te über die Landnahme in den drei altisraelitischen Geschichtswerken
   (BeihZAW 90), Berlin 1964.
   Cf. p. 12.
Mowinckel 1967
   Sigmund Mowinckel, Israels opphav og eldste historie, Oslo 1967.
   Cf. p. 12.
Müller 1978
   Hans-Peter Müller, Einige alttestamentliche Probleme zur aramäischen
   Inschrift von Dēr 'Allā, ZDPV 94 (1978), pp. 56-67.
   Cf. p. 143 (note 20).
Naveh 1967
   Joseph Naveh, The Date of the Deir 'Allā Inscription in Aramaic Script,
   IEJ 17 (1967), pp. 256-58.
   Cf. p. 103.
E. Nielsen 1950-52
   Eduard Nielsen, Jeremja og Jojakim (DTT 13 (1950), pp. 129-45) and
   Mundtlig tradition I-III (DTT 15 (1952), pp. 19-37; 88-106; 129-46). Ap-
   peared in English as Oral Tradition (1954).
   Cf. pp. 58; 135 (note 4).
E. Nielsen 1952
   Eduard Nielsen, The Righteous and the Wicked in Habaqquq, StTh 6
   (1952), pp. 54-78.
   Cf. p. 76.
E. Nielsen 1954
   Eduard Nielsen, Oral Tradition. A Modern Problem in Old Testament
   Introduction (Studies in Biblical Theology 11), London 1954.
   Cf. pp. 58; 65; 135 (note 4); 141 (note 4).
E. Nielsen 1955
   Eduard Nielsen, Shechem. A Traditio-Historical Investigation, Copen-
   hagen 1955.
   Cf. pp. 59; 88; 135 (note 4).
E. Nielsen 1965
   Eduard Nielsen, De ti Bud. En traditionshistorisk Skitse (Festskrift ud-
   givet af Københavns Universitet), København 1965 (Eng. Translation:
   The Ten Commandments in New Perspective (Studies in Biblical Theo-
   logy, Sec. Ser. 7), London 1968).
   Cf. pp. 22; 59.

E. Nielsen 1982
Eduard Nielsen, Moses and the Law, VT 32 (1982), pp. 87-98 (repr. in: Law, History and Tradition, København 1983, pp. 119-28).
Cf. p. 20.

K. Nielsen 1978
Kirsten Nielsen, Yahweh as Prosecutor and Judge. An Investigation of the Prophetic Lawsuit (Rîb-Pattern) (JSOT Suppl. Ser. 9), Sheffield 1978.
Cf. p. 63.

Nötscher 1915
Friedrich Nötscher, Die Gerechtigkeit Gottes bei den vorexilischen Propheten (Alttestamentliche Abhandlungen VI,1), Münster i. Westf. 1915.
Cf. pp. 68-70.

Norin 1977
Stig I.L. Norin, Er spaltete das Meer. Die Auszugsüberlieferung in Psalmen und Kult des alten Israel (Coniectanea Biblica. Old Testament Series 9), Lund 1977.
Cf. pp. 87; 115; 117f; 145 (notes 21f).

North 1979
Robert North, A History of Biblical Map-making (Beihefte zum Tübinger Atlas des Vorderen Orients, Reihe B, Nr. 32), Wiesbaden 1979.
Cf. p. 95.

Noth 1938
Martin Noth, Das Buch Josua (Handbuch zum Alten Testament, hrsg. von O. Eissfeldt, 1. Reihe, 7), Tübingen 1938.
Cf. p. 14.

Noth 1943
Martin Noth, Überlieferungsgeschichtliche Studien. Die sammelnden und bearbeitenden Geschichtswerke im Alten Testament (Schriften der Königsberger Gelehrten Gesellschaft, G. Kl. XVIII,2), Halle (Saale) 1943.
Cf. pp. 14f; 42; 44; 61; 85; 141 (note 6).

Noth 1948
Martin Noth, Überlieferungsgeschichte des Pentateuch, Stuttgart 1948 (cf. Noth 1972).
Cf. pp. 14; 20; 61.

Noth 1950
Martin Noth, Gott, König, Volk im Alten Testament. Eine methodologische Auseiandersetzung mit einer gegenwärtigen Forschungsrichtung, ZThK 47 (1950), pp. 157-91.
Cf. pp. 33f.

Noth 1953
Martin Noth, Das Buch Josua (Handbuch zum Alten Testament, hrsg. von O. Eissfeldt, 1. Reihe, 7), 2. Aufl., Tübingen 1953.
Cf. pp. 86; 91f; 104.

Noth 1972
Martin Noth, A History of Pentateuchal Traditions. Transl. with an Introduction by B.W. Anderson, Englewood Cliffs N.J. 1972.
Cf. p. 85.

162   *Bibliography and Index*

Nyberg 1935

H.S. Nyberg, Studien zum Hoseabuche. Zugleich ein Beitrag zur Klärung des Problems der alttestamentlichen Textkritik (Uppsala Universitets Årsskrift 1935:6), Uppsala 1935.

Cf. pp. 12; 30; 53; 135 (note 3); 141 (note 4).

Nyberg 1938

H.S. Nyberg, Studien zum Religionskampf im Alten Testament, Archiv für Religionswissenschaft 35 (1938), pp. 329-87.

Cf. p. 12.

Nyberg 1941

H.S. Nyberg, Hoseaboken. Ny översättning med anmärkningar (Uppsala Universitets Årsskrift 1941:7,2), Uppsala 1941.

Cf. p. 12.

Nyberg 1972

H.S. Nyberg, Die schwedischen Beiträge zur alttestamentlichen Forschung in diesem Jahrhundert, Congress Volume Uppsala 1971 (Suppl VT 22), Leiden 1972, pp. 1-10.

Cf. pp. 35; 137 (notes 2, 5).

Otto 1975a

Eckart Otto, Das Mazzotfest in Gilgal (BWANT 6. Folge, Heft 7), Stuttgart 1975.

Cf. p. 142 (notes 10, 12).

Otto 1975b

Eckart Otto, Sigmund Mowinckels Bedeutung für die gegenwärtige Liturgiedebatte, Jahrb. für Liturgik u. Hymnol. 19 (1975), pp. 19-36.

Cf. pp. 144 (note 1); 147 (note 1).

Ottosson 1969

Magnus Ottosson, Gilead. Tradition and History (Coniectanea Biblica. Old Testament Series 3), Lund 1969.

Cf. pp. 102; 104; 143 (note 22).

Ottosson 1981a

Magnus Ottosson, Topography and City Planning. The Extent of Jerusalem, in: ALESCO Abstracts. The First International Symposium on Palestine Antiquities, Aleppo 1981, pp. 6-7.

Cf. p. 143 (note 24).

Ottosson 1981b

Magnus Ottosson, review: Ljung 1978, Biblica 62 (1981), pp. 293-96.

Cf. p. 119.

Pedersen 1920

Johs. Pedersen, Israel I-II. Sjæleliv og Samfundsliv, København 1920 (Eng. Translation: Israel. Its Life and Culture I-II, London and Copenhagen 1926).

Cf. pp. 70; 71-73; 75-77; 79f; 86.

Pedersen 1934a

Johs. Pedersen, Israel III-IV. Hellighed og Guddommelighed, København 1934 (Eng. Translation: Israel. Its Life and Culture III-IV, London and Copenhagen 1940).

Cf. pp. 13; 16; 19.

Pedersen 1934b
Johs. Pedersen, Passahfest und Passahlegende, ZAW 52 (1934), pp. 161-75.
Cf. pp. 13; 19; 28.

Pedersen 1940
Johs. Pedersen, Canaanite and Israelite Cultus, AcOr 18 (1940), pp. 1-14.
Cf. p. 131.

Pedersen 1941
Johs. Pedersen, Die KRT Legende, Berytus 6 (1941), pp. 63-105.
Cf. p. 74.

Perlitt 1969
Lothar Perlitt, Bundestheologie im Alten Testament (WMANT 36), Neu-kirchen 1969.
Cf. pp. 22; 136 (note 8).

van der Ploeg 1947
J. van der Ploeg, Le rôle de la tradition orale dans la transmission du texte de l'Ancien Testament, RB 54 (1947), pp. 5-41.
Cf. p. 59.

Puukko 1910
A.F. Puukko, Das Deuteronomium. Eine literarkritische Untersuchung (BWANT 5), Leipzig 1910.
Cf. p. 33.

Puukko 1947
A.F. Puukko, Är den gammaltestamentliga forskningen på villovägar? Några randanmärkningar till Ivan Engnells bok "Gamla Testamentet. En traditionshistorisk inledning", Teologinen Aikakauskirja 52 (1947), pp. 64-70.
Cf. p. 33.

von Rad 1938
Gerhard von Rad, Das formgeschichtliche Problem des Hexateuchs (BWANT 4. Folge, Heft 26), Stuttgart 1938.
Cf. pp. 14; 61.

von Rad 1949-52
Gerhard von Rad, Das erste Buch Mose. Genesis (Das Alte Testament Deutsch 2-4), Göttingen 1949-52.
Cf. p. 135 (note 2).

von Rad 1950
Gerhard von Rad, "Gerechtigkeit" und "Leben" in der Kultsprache der Psalmen, in: Festschrift Alfred Bertholet zum 80. Geburtstag gewidmet, Tübingen 1950, pp. 418-37.
Cf. p. 75.

von Rad 1957
Gerhard von Rad, Theologie des Alten Testaments, Band 1: Die Theolo-gie der geschichtlichen Überlieferungen Israels, München 1957.
Cf. p. 79.

Reisner 1924
G.A. Reisner et al., Harvard Excavations at Samaria 1908-1910, I, Cam-

bridge Mass. 1924.
   Cf. p. 104.

Reiterer 1976

   F.V. Reiterer, Gerechtigkeit als Heil. *ṣdq* bei Deuterojesaja. Aussage und
   Vergleich mit der alttestamentlichen Tradition, Graz 1976.
   Cf. p. 71.

Renaud 1964

   B. Renaud, Structure et attaches littéraires de Michée IV-V (Cahiers de
   la Revue Biblique 2), Paris 1964.
   Cf. p. 65.

Renaud 1977

   B. Renaud, La formation du livre de Michée. Tradition et Actualisation
   (Etudes bibliques), Paris 1977.
   Cf. p. 65.

Rendtorff 1966

   Rolf Rendtorff, Litterärkritik och traditionshistoria, SEÅ 31 (1966),
   pp. 1-20.
   Cf. pp. 26; 144 (note 5).

Rendtorff 1975

   Rolf Rendtorff, Der "Jahwist" als Theologe? Zum Dilemma der Penta-
   teuchkritik, Congress Volume Edinburgh 1974 (SupplVT 28), Leiden
   1975, pp. 158-66.
   Cf. p. 136 (note 10).

Rendtorff 1977

   Rolf Rendtorff, Das überlieferungsgeschichtliche Problem des Pentateuch
   (BeihZAW 147), Berlin 1977.
   Cf. pp. 17; 24; 26-28.

Richter 1966

   W. Richter, review: Carlson 1964, BZ N.F. 10 (1966), pp. 138-39.
   Cf. p. 43.

Richter 1971

   W. Richter, Exegese als Literaturwissenschaft. Entwurf einer alttestamentlichen Literaturtheorie und Methodologie, Göttingen 1971.
   Cf. p. 140 (note 51).

Ringgren 1947

   Helmer Ringgren, Word and Wisdom. Studies in the Hypostatization of
   Divine Qualities and Functions in the Ancient Near East, Lund 1947.
   Cf. pp. 74; 76.

Ringgren 1949

   Helmer Ringgren, Oral and Written Transmission in the O.T. Some Observations, StTh 3 (1949), pp. 34-59.
   Cf. pp. 59; 112f; 145 (note 14).

Ringgren 1957

   Helmer Ringgren, Psaltarens fromhet, Stockholm 1957.
   Cf. pp. 112; 115.

Ringgren 1963
    Helmer Ringgren, Israelitische Religion (Die Religionen der Menschheit 26), Stuttgart 1963.
        Cf. p. 79.

Ringgren 1966
    Helmer Ringgren, Literarkritik, Formgeschichte, Überlieferungsgeschichte. Erwägungen zur Methodenfrage der alttestamentlichen Exegese, ThLz 91 (1966), cols. 641-50.
        Cf. pp. 17; 51; 137 (note 10); 144 (note 5).

Ringgren 1969
    Helmer Ringgren, Foreword, in: Engnell 1969, pp. ix-xi.
        Cf. p. 137 (notes 1, 3, 13).

Ringgren 1977
    Helmer Ringgren, Bileam och inskriften från Deir 'Allā, RoB 36 (1977), pp. 85-89.
        Cf. p. 143 (note 19).

Ritschl 1900
    Albrecht Ritschl, Die christliche Lehre von der Rechtfertigung und Versöhnung, 4. Aufl., Bonn 1895-1903 (Bd. 2: Der biblische Stoff der Lehre, 4. Aufl., Bonn 1900).
        Cf. pp. 70f.

Ruh 1981
    Hans Ruh, Gerechtigkeitstheorien, in: Gerechtigkeit. Themen der Sozialethik, hrsg. von Armin Wildermuth und Alfred Jäger, Tübingen 1981, pp. 55-69.
        Cf. p. 67.

Sæbø 1974
    Magne Sæbø, Grenzbeschreibung und Landideal im Alten Testament. Mit besonderer Berücksichtigung der *min-'ad*-Formel, ZDPV 90 (1974), pp. 14-37.
        Cf. p. 142 (note 14).

Sæbø 1978
    Magne Sæbø, Vom Grossreich zum Weltreich. Erwägungen zu Pss. lxxii 8, lxxxix 26; Sach. ix 10b, VT 28 (1978), pp. 83-91.
        Cf. p. 142 (note 14).

Sæbø 1981
    Magne Sæbø, Priestertheologie und Priesterschrift. Zur Eigenart der priesterlichen Schicht im Pentateuch, Congress Volume Vienna 1980 (SupplVT 32), Leiden 1981, pp. 357-74.
        Cf. p. 135 (note 7).

Schmid 1968
    H.H. Schmid, Gerechtigkeit als Weltordnung. Hintergrund und Geschichte des alttestamentlichen Gerechtigkeitsbegriffes (Beiträge z. hist. Theologie 40), Tübingen 1968.
        Cf. p. 79.

Schmid 1976

H.H. Schmid, Der sogenannte Jahwist. Beobachtungen und Fragen zur Pentateuchforschung, Zürich 1976.
   Cf. pp. 24-26.
Schmid 1981

H.H. Schmid, Auf der Suche nach neuen Perspektiven für die Pentateuchforschung, Congress Volume Vienna 1980 (SupplVT 32), Leiden 1981, pp. 375-94.
   Cf. p. 26.
Schmidt 1966

Werner H. Schmidt, Königtum Gottes in Ugarit und Israel. Zur Herkunft der Königsprädikation Jahwes (BeihZAW 80), 2. neu bearbeitete Auflage, Berlin 1966.
   Cf. p. 146 (note 24).
Schmitt 1977

Armin Schmitt, Die Totenerweckung in 1 Kön. XVII 17-24. Eine form- und gattungskritische Untersuchung, VT 27 (1977), pp. 454-74.
   Cf. p. 142 (note 11).
Van Seters 1975

John Van Seters, Abraham in History and Tradition, New Haven 1975.
   Cf. p. 60.
Simons 1947

J. Simons, Two Connected Problems Relating to the Israelite Settlement in Transjordan, PEQ 79 (1947), pp. 27-39; 87-101.
   Cf. p. 103.
Skinner 1922

John Skinner, Prophecy and Religion. Studies in the Life of Jeremiah, Cambridge 1922.
   Cf. p. 66.
Smend 1978

Rudolf Smend, Die Entstehung des Alten Testament (Theologische Wissenschaft 1), Stuttgart 1978.
   Cf. p. 17.
Snaith 1978

N.H. Snaith, The Altar at Gilgal: Joshua XXII 23-29, VT 28 (1978), pp. 330-35.
   Cf. p. 102.
Soggin 1972

J.A. Soggin, Joshua. A Commentary, London 1972.
   Cf. p. 92.
Springer 1979

Simone Springer, Neuinterpretation im Alten Testament. Untersucht an den Themenkreisen des Herbstfestes und der Königspsalmen in Israel (Stuttgarter Biblische Beiträge), Stuttgart 1979.
   Cf. pp. 115-117; 145 (notes 19f).

Steck 1972
Odil Hannes Steck, Friedensvorstellungen im alten Jerusalem (Theologische Studien 111), Zürich 1972.
Cf. p. 124.

Tengström 1976
Sven Tengström, Die Hezateucherzählung. Eine literaturgeschichtliche Studie (Coniectanea Biblica. Old Testament Series 7), Lund 1976.
Cf. pp. 22; 142 (note 9).

Tengström 1982
Sven Tengström, Die Toledotformel und die literarische Struktur der priesterlichen Erweiterungsschicht im Pentateuch (Coniectanea Biblica. Old Testament Series 17), Lund 1982.
Cf. pp. 23; 142 (note 9).

Veijola 1975
Timo Veijola, Die ewige Dynastie. David und die Entstehung seiner Dynastie nach der deuteronomistischen Darstellung (AASF Ser. B Tom. 193), Helsinki 1975.
Cf. pp. 45; 47; 139 (note 41); 140 (notes 47, 49).

Veijola 1979
Timo Veijola, Salomo – der Erstgeborene Bathsebas, in: Studies in the Historical Books of the Old Testament, ed. J.A. Emerton (SupplVT 30), Leiden 1979, pp. 230-50.
Cf. p. 49.

Veijola 1982
Timo Veijola, Verheissung in der Krise. Studien zur Literatur und Theologie der Exilszeit anhand des 89. Psalms (AASF Ser. B Tom. 220), Helsinki 1982.
Cf. pp. 38-41; 45; 122f; 138 (notes 24, 26, 29, 32); 139 (notes 33, 41, 43).

Watters 1976
W.R. Watters, Formula Criticism and the Poetry of the Old Testament (BeihZAW 138), Berlin 1976.
Cf. pp. 120; 122; 146 (note 27).

Weinfeld 1972
Moshe Weinfeld, Deuteronomy and the Deuteronomic School, Oxford 1972.
Cf. p. 141 (note 7).

Weiser 1950
Artur Weiser, Die Psalmen (ATD 14/15), Göttingen 1950.
Cf. pp. 76; 79.

Weiser 1966
Artur Weiser, Die Legitimation des Königs David. Zur Eigenart und Entstehung der sogen. Geschichte von Davids Aufstieg. VT 16 (1966), pp. 325-54.
Cf. p. 47.

Wellhausen 1894
Julius Wellhausen, Israelitische und jüdische Geschichte, Berlin 1894.
Cf. p. 13.

Wellhausen 1899
Julius Wellhausen, Die Composition des Hexateuchs und der historischen Bücher des Alten Testaments, 3. Aufl., Berlin 1899.
   Cf. p. 44.
Westermann 1961
Claus Westermann, Das Loben Gottes in den Psalmen, 2. Auflage, Göttingen 1961.
   Cf. pp. 124; 147 (note 31).
Widengren 1948
Geo Widengren, Literary and Psychological Aspects of the Hebrew Prophets (Uppsala Universitets Årsskrift 1948:10), Uppsala 1948.
   Cf. pp. 30; 59.
Widengren 1959
Geo Widengren, Oral Tradition and Written Literature among the Hebrews in the Light of Arabic Evidence with Special Regard to Prose Narratives, AcOr 23 (1959), pp. 201-62.
   Cf. pp. 30; 60; 141 (note 4).
Wilcoxen 1968
J.A. Wilcoxen, Narrative Structure and Cult Legend. A Study of Joshua 1-6, in: Transitions in Biblical Scholarship, ed. J.C. Rylaarsdam, Chicago 1968, pp. 43-70.
   Cf. p. 89.
Wolff 1953
Hans Walter Wolff, "Wissen um Gott" bei Hosea als Urform von Theologie, EvTh 12 (1952-53), pp. 533-54.
   Cf. p. 79.
Wolff 1961
Hans Walter Wolff, Dodekapropheton 1. Hosea (BK XIV/1), Neukirchen 1961.
   Cf. pp. 61f.
Würthwein 1974
Ernst Würthwein, Die Erzählung von der Thronfolge Davids – theologische oder politische Geschichtsschreibung? (Theologische Studien 115), Zürich 1974.
   Cf. pp. 49; 140 (note 49).
Yadin 1961
Yigael Yadin, Ancient Judaean Weights and the Date of the Samaria Ostraca, Scripta Hierosolymitana 8 (1961), pp. 9-25.
   Cf. p. 104.
Zobel 1973
Hans-Jürgen Zobel, $^{a}r\bar{o}n$, ThWAT I, Stuttgart 1973, cols. 391-404.
   Cf. p. 93.
van Zyl 1960
A.H. van Zyl, The Moabites (Pretoria Oriental Series, ed. A. van Selms, vol. 3), Leiden 1960.
   Cf. p. 101.

PARTICIPANTS FROM THE THEOLOGICAL FACULTIES OF:

LUND
Erik Aurelius
Gillis Gerleman
Sten Hidal
Bo Johnson
Eva Strömberg Krantz
Frederik Lindström
Tryggve Mettinger
Stig Norin

UPPSALA
Bertil Albrektson
Gunnel André
Agge Carlson
Inger Ljung
Magnus Ottosson
Helmer Ringgren
Per Stille
Sven Tengström

CHICAGO
Gösta W. Ahlström

OSLO
Hans M. Barstad
Martin R. Hauge
Arvid S. Kapelrud

Congregational Faculty:
Anders J. Bjørndalen
Magne Sæbø
Arvid Tångberg
Karl William Weyde

HELSINKI
Anneli Aejmelaeus
Ilmari Soisalon-Soininen
Timo Veijola

ÅBO
Karl-Johan Illman
Nils Martola
Roger Syrén

REYKJAVIK
Thorir Thordarson

KØBENHAVN
Bodil Ejrnæs
Heike Friis
Jakob Grønbæk
Svend Holm-Nielsen
Arne Munk
Eduard Nielsen
Kjeld Nielsen
Karin Friis Plum
John Strange

AARHUS
Frederick Cryer
Knud Jeppesen
Niels Peter Lemche
Hans Aage Mink
Bent Mogensen
Kirsten Nielsen
Benedikt Otzen
Carsten Vang

Secretariate:
Birgit Herman Hansen
Søren Jensen
Else Kragelund

169